Acclaim for *Building a Successful Selling Organization*

"A must-read for anyone interested in building a world-class sales organization. Art Wilson and the CPS team set out a clear action-able agenda. If you are or want to be a leader in your sales organization, read this book now!"

—Jerry Gauche
Senior Vice President, Sales and Marketing
National Oilwell Varco, Inc.

"Art Wilson and his team have actually walked in our shoes. Their consolidated knowledge and experience helped to broaden our thinking, resulting in better partnerships with our customers and our strategic suppliers as well. This book is about building sustainable relationships."

—Gene Batchelder
Chief Information Officer and Senior Vice
President of Administration
ConocoPhillips

"The methodologies taught by Art Wilson and his Critical Path Strategies team of pros enabled ordinary sales teams to achieve extraordinary results every time I have used them. Putting these methods into book form should make CPS a household name in American businesses."

—Charles Ansley
Chief Executive Officer and President
Symon Communications, Inc.

"Art and his partners at Critical Path Strategies are quintessential sales professionals. Their many years of experience, strong customer relationships, and disciplined sales processes and strategies make them subject-matter experts."

—Jim Steele
President
Salesforce.com

"Art Wilson is an accomplished and well-respected sales leader. In his book, *Building a Successful Selling Organization*, he and his partners artfully demystify the how-to process for creating a results-driven sales team."

—William (Bill) J. Smith, III
General Manager
IBM Global Financing—Americas

"As a sales leader, I'm always trying to use the very best consultative sales process and ensure that my team can execute with it. This is very difficult to do with a large organization, but Art Wilson and the CPS team make it happen. With a combination of simple-to-use tools, hands-on facilitation, and 'war stories' our sales reps can put into action, Art and his colleagues make selling into large accounts a definable, repeatable, results-oriented process. Having seen Art in action for more than 18 years, I know this works, and *Building a Successful Selling Organization* will show you how."

—Eddie Marshall
General Manager, South Central District
Microsoft Corporation

"Art Wilson and his colleagues are nothing less than sales and marketing geniuses! But the best part is their ability to get across leading-edge and revolutionary concepts, no matter the audience. If you want a breakthrough this year in your sales and marketing results, read this book now!"

—Germaine Porché and Jed Niederer
Cofounders, Eagle's View Systems, Inc.
Coauthors, *Coach Anyone About Anything*

"Keeping it simple, Art Wilson and his team really get it. They have encapsulated in this book and in their process what took me over 30 years to learn the hard way. I have applied these techniques in different companies, industries, geographies, and cultures with the same result...they simply work!"

—Bill LaRosa
Corporate Vice President
Global Account Sales and Marketing
AMD

"I have known Art Wilson for 25-plus years. He worked for me at IBM and was an outstanding sales executive. Art is methodical, customer-oriented, and has the tenacity of a bulldog! He makes things happen for the mutual benefit of the customer and the company!"

—Les Lesniak
Senior Vice President, Corporate
Siemens Communications, Enterprise Networks

"Reading Art Wilson's book, *Building a Successful Selling Organization*, provides unique insight into the processes and disciplines needed to effectively manage a customer-facing organization, regardless of the product line. It provides a road map for strengthening sales teams to meet challenges of today's ever-changing markets. I recommend it for every sales manager and team leader, regardless of their level in the organization."

—R. G. (Bob) Wallace
retired Executive Vice President
Phillips Petroleum and President,
Phillips 66 Company

"Art Wilson and the Critical Path Strategies team have developed an effective sales methodology that is a winner. In *Building a Successful Selling Organization*, Art takes 30 years of creating win-win customer relationships, and shows you how to build powerful partnerships that transform your business."

—Kevin Weiss
Executive Vice President, Customer Operations
McAfee, Inc.

"Critical Path Strategies has been a leader in sales strategy and development for many years. Founder Art Wilson and his partners are world-class in developing and managing winning sales strategies. Your selling teams and your customers will benefit greatly from their insights and approaches. I highly recommend this book as the blueprint for developing a disciplined and successful sales team."

—David M. Ernsberger
President, Ernsberger Partnerships, Inc. and
retired Group Vice President of Worldwide Sales and Service,
IBM Technology Group

"Art Wilson is the real deal when it comes to selling. In *Building a Successful Selling Organization*, Art and his partners at Critical Path Strategies have taken decades of sales experience and condensed them into an easy-to-read, 'how-to' book. Anyone interested in creating a world-class sales force should read this book."

—Pat Cathey
President
ACS North America

"Today, more than ever, relationships drive value in business. In *Building a Successful Selling Organization*, Art Wilson shares his secrets for producing high-performing sales teams that take ownership of the relationship through disciplined accountability. Every sales team can benefit from the real-world insights of successful sales executives."

—Jan Twombly and Jeff Shuman
Cofounders, The Rhythm of Business, Inc.
Coauthors, *Collaborative Communities: Partnering for
Profit in the Networked Economy*

"As CSO of a company that made 40-plus acquisitions within an eight-year period, I was faced with the daunting task of creating a common process out of 40 legacy methodologies around sales. Art and the CPS professionals provided us with a blueprint of basic fundamentals needed to create *sales process*, a plan for creating consistent execution and repeatable sustainable behaviors, and knowledge of how to measure customer-focused sales performance. They allowed us to 'enculturate' a real and simple sales process to follow. They are an extremely talented group who deliver exemplary results.

—Cornelius Dupré
Chairman
Venture Transport Logistics

"I have known Art for over 12 years. His advice and counsel in building, operating, and improving sales teams have been invaluable. In *Building a Successful Selling Organization*, Art and his partners have taken a lifetime of knowledge and experience and simplified it into an actionable book. Keep this one close; you will be reaching for it several times a week."

—Alex Shootman
Executive Vice President of Sales and Marketing
TeleTech

Building a Successful
Selling Organization

Building a Successful Selling Organization

The Critical Path to Extraordinary Results

Art Wilson, Founder
Critical Path Strategies, Inc.

With Mike Morton, Mike Higgins,
and Ken Evans

iUniverse, Inc.
New York Lincoln Shanghai

Building a Successful Selling Organization
The Critical Path to Extraordinary Results

Copyright © 2005 by Art Wilson

All rights reserved. No part of this book may be used or reproduced by any means, graphic, electronic, or mechanical, including photocopying, recording, taping or by any information storage retrieval system without the written permission of the publisher except in the case of brief quotations embodied in critical articles and reviews.

iUniverse books may be ordered through booksellers or by contacting:

iUniverse
2021 Pine Lake Road, Suite 100
Lincoln, NE 68512
www.iuniverse.com
1-800-Authors (1-800-288-4677)

ISBN-13: 978-0-595-36163-2 (pbk)
ISBN-13: 978-0-595-67343-8 (cloth)
ISBN-13: 978-0-595-80607-2 (ebk)
ISBN-10: 0-595-36163-3 (pbk)
ISBN-10: 0-595-67343-0 (cloth)
ISBN-10: 0-595-80607-4 (ebk)

Printed in the United States of America

Contents

Part 2. Build a Foundation for Results

Part 3. Strengthen the Sales Culture

Part 4. Instill Sales Leadership Rhythm and Coaching

Acknowledgments

Including several unsuccessful starts, I have been working on this book for 12 years, but it is the creation of many minds. Yes, it is a compilation of insights, observations, and convictions gleaned during my 30-plus years of experience selling, leading, and consulting for some of the world's most extraordinary companies. But it primarily reflects the brilliance of the dynamic and inspirational executives with whom it has been my good fortune to work. It was under their tutelage that I first survived each of my sales and sales leadership positions and then thrived, and it was their best practices that honed my personal effectiveness. For that, they have my respect, admiration, and gratitude.

The following people made meaningful contributions to the creation of this book. Were it not for their commitment, persistence, patience, and encouragement, this book would still be a 1,000-page document residing on my laptop. For their gifts of collaboration and encouragement, they have my heartfelt appreciation.

- To the leadership at IBM, for instilling in me a selling and leadership culture that served me well while in their employ, enabled me to give birth to Critical Path Strategies (CPS), and continues to indirectly influence our successful relationships with clients.

- To Germaine Porché and Jed Niederer, who coached me through the first stages of development of this book.

- To Margaret Tanaszi, the wonderful book doctor who helped organize my thoughts and early drafts during the last three years of work on this book. She helped provide a springboard for the finished product.

- To former CPS partners Ann Perrin, for her marketing wizardry, significant contributions to CPS and this book, and continuing commitment to what we do, and Don Pearson, for his commitment to CPS since 1993 through many engagements with our clients.

- To the many client executives we interviewed and who reviewed early drafts of this book, including Jerry Gauche, Gene Batchelder, Charles Ansley, Bob Wallace, Dave Ernsberger, Cornelius Dupré, and Alex Shootman. We benefited greatly from their thoughtful and incisive comments.

- To the executive leadership of our 100-plus clients, who have entrusted their sales organizations to us to do what we love to do.

- To my long-time partners Mary Ann Costello and Jim Ryan and my other committed colleagues at Critical Path Strategies, for their dedication, uncommon loyalty, and world-class professionalism.

- To Nancy Coger, for her editorial assistance and sense of quality, central to producing this book and CPS' intellectual property material for the last eight years.

- To Jeanne Buchanan, for her creative energy. She finally got this book out the door.

And please indulge these particularly personal acknowledgements.

- To my partners in business and in writing this book, Mike Morton, Mike Higgins, and Ken Evans. How lucky I am to work side-by-side with them. They each bring an incredible dimension to my life. I am equally grateful to their spouses and children. They have been great supporters of our life's work in spite of our many absences.

- To my wonderful wife Kathy, and my four children, Jeff, Amy, Ann, and Jill. Their positive spirit and ever-present encouragement keep me moving forward.

- And last, but not least, to my grandpa, Arthur Fabra, who demonstrated to me at an early age what it means to serve people by selling them something they need, and to my grandma, Amy Fabra, who encouraged her grandchildren and gave us more confidence than we ever had in ourselves.

Foreword

Like many of you, I did not start in sales. I graduated with a degree in business from the University of Texas and went to work as a computer programmer. IBM hired me in 1969 to be a systems engineer, or so I thought. Shortly after my arrival, my branch manager pulled me aside and informed me that I would become a salesperson. I knew nothing of selling, but I had few other job options.

Shortly after this conversation, I met with Bill Barley, my first sales manager. Scared to death of this new job, I closed the door and asked him for one idea that could help me survive, then potentially excel, in my suddenly imposed sales career. He strongly suggested that I identify some of the most successful salespeople within IBM, study their selling habits, and adapt their approaches to suit my style. What a gift this suggestion turned out to be!

I gained a competitive edge early on by applying the winning ways of superior salespeople. I learned that successful sales professionals share definable characteristics that serve them, in good times and bad. By being in IBM's very strong sales leadership culture, and proactively studying and adopting these effective, field-proven operating practices from people I identified, I gained insight and ideas that led to extraordinary results I would otherwise never have achieved. I did not know it at the time, but this watch, learn, and emulate technique would become the platform for my success and for many people I have been honored to work with. I have been a student of best-practices-based selling organizations and sales leaders ever since.

Identifying and codifying best practices is not a new idea. The technique is widely understood and adopted, because it is remarkably effective. Today, the United Nations has a group dedicated to best practices in peacekeeping. The United States Secret Service has a policy on best practices for seizing electronic evidence. There is a Center for Best Practices in Early Childhood. Fortune 500 companies, spanning a variety of industries, have known the value of best-practice benchmarking. While most are anecdotal, I believe you will find the approaches in this book quite systematic, pragmatic, and useful.

I had the opportunity to take early retirement from IBM while I was still quite young. Thanks to IBM and a number of clients who committed to work with me if I would develop a process to transfer best practices to their selling organizations, I was able to dedicate myself to creating the basis of a very successful consulting practice that has worked with 13,000-plus professionals in over 100 companies, from one-person firms to Fortune 100 corporations.

Critical Path Strategies, Inc. now has over 25 wonderful, dedicated employees who help our clients deliver extraordinary results globally to their customers. Many of our clients do not have years to spend on the watch-and-learn process that I did, nor are they fortunate enough to be in companies with incredibly strong sales and sales leadership cultures. With our clients, we have identified and systematized agendas, cultures, processes, and disciplines that consistently deliver improvements in sales productivity and profits.

Since I started this business in 1992, many of our clients have encouraged us to present the building blocks of a successful selling organization. The demands of a busy consulting business have made that a laborious and intermittent process. But with the help of my partners, associates, and many of our clients, I have captured in this book what we have learned over decades of selling and teaching others to sell. It incorporates best practices in a framework for sales organization leadership, from the CEO to leaders of sales teams, who desire to significantly improve their performance. Unlike the hundreds of books about selling that are on the market, this is a logical framework for sales leaders at every level who want to generate extraordinary results for their company's stakeholders.

My friend, Bob Wallace, a lifelong sales and marketing professional who became president of Phillips 66, told me that his career might have been even more successful if he had learned our methodology early on. "If, as a young sales manager, I could have had this book to explain what a real sales management process is, I would have produced significantly better results in each of my positions. I did not know what I did not know until I was one or two levels above each position."

The clients who measure the results of our work typically see 100 to 500 times our fees in revenue increases. It has been gratifying for all of us at CPS to see our clients achieve such significant results based on our work. With the publication of this book, we now have a new way to pass on our blueprint for selling organization success.

Art Wilson

Art Wilson
Founder, Critical Path Strategies, Inc.

Preface

More than 10 years ago, Critical Path Strategies began receiving requests from clients and associates to write a comprehensive book about how to create and lead a successful selling organization.

Founded in 1992, CPS has consulted with over 100 companies, partnering with chief executive officers and chief sales officers, their sales leadership, their distribution channels, their customers, and—in some cases—their strategic suppliers. CPS teams have been honored to meet and work with thousands of sales leaders and their customers in many ways—from team planning sessions to training, process consulting, customer relationship management (CRM) implementation, and coaching on sales opportunities. In all cases, we utilized a proven methodology and set of tools to guide teams through thought processes that help change behavior and lead to extraordinary results.

Because of our extensive sales leadership experience, many clients engaged us to become an integral part of their organization or to assume an interim organizational management role. In addition, we have sponsored and been asked to participate in several research projects concerning successful sales organizations and have written over 50 articles and white papers.

Why did we write this book now? Beginning in 2000, we began to observe some pervasive changes emerging in many of our clients' sales environments that would require dramatically different responses from those of the past. Many of our clients are coming to similar conclusions regarding these dramatic sales environment changes.

- Organizations continue to post the same unacceptable sales results when they react to problems the way they have in the past.

- The real answer is not just in training, but rather in intentionally working with the sales management team to take primary ownership of results, and the fundamental behavior of the sales force after they go through training.

- We need to apply proven practices, which govern other parts of our business, to our sales organization. We need a more confident view of the future and issues that must be addressed before they become unfixable.

While there are thousands of books on the subject of sales and selling, we have found none targeted at chief sales officers, their sales leadership, and their agendas for growth. This book is particularly aimed at sales leadership of mid-sized to large companies where a short list of critical customer relationships determines the ultimate success of the organization as a whole.

One of the most interesting things we have observed recently is how similar the process and sales management solution is in today's sales environment for all sizes of sales organizations—from the very small (10 to 50) to the very large (1,000-plus). We attribute this trend to four things.

1. Technology and globalization provide extensive visibility of products and services. Small and large sales forces are now competing for many of the same sales and relationships. Even a small firm with strong marketing, sales pipeline management, resource planning, account management, and sales forecasting practices can be successful.

2. CRM software with high functionality is more available to sales organizations of all sizes, and it is easy to personalize, implement, and use.

3. In the 1990s, many consulting and sales organizations (CPS and its clients included) focused research on capturing and codifying the practices of the best-of-the-best salespeople. This data, primarily from top-performing large sales organizations, has trickled down to smaller firms, generating better results than those of larger counterparts.

4. And, finally, the focus on developing consistent management processes and accountability for driving the attendant behavior change enables a smaller competitor to win over a slumbering giant.

We believe that our experience and learnings in addressing these changing environmental drivers is universally relevant to all sales organizations and will leverage your experience.

Building a Successful Selling Organization is presented in four parts.

1>	Acknowledge the Current Selling Environment	Chapters 1–3
2>	Build a Foundation for Results	Chapters 4–8
3>	Strengthen the Sales Culture	Chapters 9–11
4>	Instill Sales Leadership Rhythm and Coaching	Chapters 12–14

Part 1 focuses on acknowledging that something in the selling environment has changed, and determining what functions of the sales agenda require the most improvement.

Part 2 helps sales leadership lay a foundation for results. First and foremost is a discussion about becoming customer centric in the way we interact with customers, which is fundamental to a sales organization's success.

Part 3 explores taking the CSO agenda one click deeper, effectively organizing for account management execution and attendant relationship management issues and best practices.

Part 4 discusses "making it stick" with management rhythm and a coaching culture.

Note: Anecdotes in this book are true. In some cases, the names of clients have been changed.

Part 1.
Acknowledge the Current Selling Environment

Why is it that some sales leaders and selling organizations always seem to be prepared for unforeseen changes in the marketplace, almost like they had a crystal ball, while others seem to be in constant reaction mode?

For decades sales leaders have dealt with the types of issues being experienced today, with one fundamental difference. Because of the many changes in the business environment, it is extremely difficult to forecast business cycles in terms of the timing, direction (up or down), rate of change, and duration.

Great leaders face the reality of the selling environment. They create an agenda for their organization that addresses the current environment, while focusing on several key areas that will allow them to take advantage of opportunities afforded them during the coming year.

The following three chapters are about acknowledging the current reality of the marketplace—from the customer, competition, partner, and selling organization perspective—and creating and activating a sales agenda in a way that gets traction and prepares the organization for success in the current selling environment.

The reality of unforecastable change is with us from now on. Squarely facing the reality of today while thinking long-term and focusing the organization on short-term action has never been more important. Those leaders who do not prepare to successfully deal with change are destined to spend their time reacting to others' agendas.

1

Face Reality

Change is the law of life and those who look only to the past or present are certain to miss the future.

—John F. Kennedy

Sales organizations that operate under strategic sales principles are able to deliver predictable, sustainable results based on high-value activities focused on customer success. Success lies in the hands of many.

Sales organizations that operate by seat-of-the-pants, tactical reactions to the marketplace are doomed to be at the mercy of others' agendas. Their success lies in the hands of a few.

The gap between the strategic principles and tactical reactions represents the cost of not investing in strategic sales leadership. A typical situation might play out as follows.

> The Monday morning sales meeting begins as usual, but this time, the news is grim. Results are disappointing, the sales opportunity pipeline is anemic, and the number of customer complaints has skyrocketed. There is anxiety in the chief sales officer's voice and people around the room have a look of quiet consternation.
>
> Someone suggests a quick-fix tactical course of action. Most people know that another short-term fix for a long-standing problem will not improve results. But beyond that, they do not know what happened. As the Buffalo Springfield song says, *"Something's happening here, though what it is ain't exactly clear."*

There are further complications. The morning news brings word of a possible new regulatory framework that will limit the company's flexibility, and of a merger of two of the company's competitors that will produce a giant in the industry. These circumstances cast a long shadow on the company's already shaky fortunes.

This is a sales organization at the mercy of other people's agendas. It does not have fixes for its problems, nor is it clear what led to those problems. The company's sales machine has been coasting, going with the flow, and has just taken a plunge into whitewater.

Without resetting strategy and committing to a strategic plan of action, the selling organization places itself—and the company—at serious risk. It is scrambling to stay afloat.

Echoes of a Common Problem

Consider the ramifications and noise we might hear from the stakeholders of this selling organization.

The Customer Executive

The customers of this selling organization are under incredible pressure. They have a hunger to improve their efficiency and effectiveness, but must reduce expenses and increase revenue. Since they have only finite resources on which to draw, they are acutely responsive to whatever they think will give them an advantage in a fierce market. If you asked customer executives what causes them heartburn, you might hear the following response.

> We are working in a global economy. We are under extreme pressure from our shareholders and the marketplace. There is so much that we cannot control, and so much that affects us. It is difficult to forecast the ups and downs of the marketplace, but we need to be better prepared to respond to both of these conditions. We really need to use strategic suppliers effectively to compete, but we have little organizational experience in getting the most out of them.

The Selling Company Chief Executive Officer

The selling company CEO is caught in circumstances similar to the customers he serves. He has squeezed the productivity line, but has struggled with the top line. Risk factors have increased. There is less certainty about what course is the best to pursue. He wants to be able to count on sales to help him do some reliable business planning. Here is what a typical CEO might say.

> We are being commoditized in the marketplace by customers and competitors. To make things worse, we are not just competing for products and services, but also for a share of customer budgets. And my biggest frustration? I cannot depend on sales forecasts to plan and run our business.

The Chief Sales Officer

The CSO must harness the talents of the selling organization to deliver growth. Specifically, growth that will sustain customer relationships. At the same time, he needs the diplomatic skills of a United Nations envoy to gain the commitment and participation of company peers for sales investments. What is the chief sales officer thinking?

> We spend most of our time reacting to competitors or to customer buying processes instead of being proactive. Our sales teams focus only on making quarter-to-quarter targets, so I cannot make much headway on our long-term sales strategy. To our customers, we look like multiple companies. There is no cohesive go-to-market strategy among various groups, and there is no real recognition of value sold to the customer and valued delivered.

The Sales Manager

The first-line sales manager is perhaps in the most difficult position in the company. This person inevitably has to respond to expectations for results and direction from superiors, while actively helping sales teams do their jobs and keep up with customers, quality issues, and of course, the competition. In addition, the sales manager must develop a pipeline of sales opportunities to keep the revenue engine running. The following are typical sales manager issues.

> My job is to lead my team to make the company's strategy a reality with the customers we are assigned. That means making the numbers every quarter. The problem is that the market has changed and what used to work is not working anymore. To make matters worse, our whole company is neurotic, almost as neurotic as my customers!

The Salesperson

The salespeople in the selling organization often struggle with mixed messages from management and conflicting incentives or requirements about what they are supposed to be doing.

> They do not have a clue! I spend 80 percent of my time reacting to customer problems, internal reporting, and forecasting demands. They change my territory regularly, which does not allow me to establish solid customer relationships. I get little helpful direction and no coaching. Besides, the way I am compensated does not match what they say they would like me to do. I am doing things that do not make business sense to our customers or our company. My resume is on the street.

What is happening here? We think these echoes have much to do with the big changes that have occurred over the last decade or so in the selling environment. People within most selling organizations today have too much to do. What they have to do is more complex than ever. Many are chasing too many targets with too few resources and do not have the experience necessary to make the best use of their time.

Also, with customer demands for supply chain management and much shorter product life cycles, the selling organization has become reliant on a much broader range of people in specialized, non-sales functions, including company executives. Without their active support, the selling organization cannot function effectively.

In our strategic account management workshops, we often ask salespeople to identify the biggest issues that they have with their customers, and that their customers have with them. Some behaviors appear with regularity in the buying-selling culture—even around potentially high-value customer/supplier relationships. Three of the most common issues indicated by our clients are price pressure, relationships, and self-interest. Here are some of the things we hear from our clients' sales organizations, and what their customers are saying about these issues.

Seller/Buyer Issues

Seller/Buyer Issue	Customer	Sales Organization
Price Pressure	Our customers are pressing us to be faster, cheaper, and better, and we have to drive those savings through our suppliers.	Our customers, especially the largest ones, want the same or better products and solutions, plus no extras, for a price that puts us in a difficult position. We either address customer needs and not make a profit, or not get the business.
Relationships as Needed	Our key suppliers are essential to our success, but they are available only when we buy something.	We do not have time to invest in relationships unless we see specific short-term sales opportunities that will help us make our quota. Besides, they will change my customer assignments next year anyway.
Self-Interest	The purchasing organization does not add value in a way that helps me use suppliers to make my revenue, total cost of operations, and risk-management targets. They do a nice job of hammering them for the best deal.	Teaming with others in my customer-facing organization is important to customer satisfaction and future business, but only if it helps me make my numbers now.

Selling Organization Issues

What are some of the major shifts in the selling environment?

Initiative overload. In a sales planning workshop we conducted with the sales organization of a prominent U.S.-based multinational firm, we discovered a striking example of this trauma to selling organizations. We asked 100 workshop participants to identify key areas on which they planned to focus their efforts in the next quarter. They identified 62 different types of internal initiatives! They told us they expected to spend 90 percent of their time in the next quarter on these initiatives. This is a neurotic organization. What about the customer?

What are some root causes for this turbulence? A lot of them have to do with the power shift from seller to buyers.

Access to information. With the Internet, buyers have access to and demand more transparency. Customers have tools to access business information, challenge standard practices, and demand changes to the design and delivery of products and services. While more businesses can reach customers more easily and in more ways than ever before, this also gives customers enormous power to vet prices, offerings, and value provided by vendors. The result is that customers have become much better at managing procurement of products and services.

Tighter processes. Both buyers and sellers have better processes—more targeted, connected, and streamlined, and even benchmarked. Mergers and acquisitions have lowered costs through consolidation. They have also spurred a trend among buyers to narrow the range of suppliers, and seek price advantages by commoditizing purchases. Suppliers also favor aggregation of products into larger, long-term contracts in order to get a bigger slice of the buyer's pie. Who would have ever thought that customers would be conducting online, reverse auctions for million-dollar product or services acquisitions?

Shorter buying cycles. The buying cycle has virtually collapsed into ever-shorter periods. People are thinking in quarterly bottom-line terms, and superiors are demanding to know specific impacts expected from these investments. Every investment is scrutinized and measured for value impact. Value life cycles are measured in months, not years.

Out-of-the-blue competitors. Technology and globalization are allowing new competitors to join the fray every day.

More people are involved in selling activity. Nearly everything about the selling environment has become more complex. The selling environment now involves many more functions. The people on whom sales leaders rely may or may not report to them, and for various accounts or projects, they will be different people.

Economic heat. The dynamics of our economy and markets are intensifying. Customers as well as sales organizations are bombarded with external pressures and are combating them in myriad ways. No wonder we observe what may amount to chaotic and dysfunctional behavior. The engagement landscape between salesperson and customer has never been more complex.

Sales loyalty. Selling organizations of the past could reasonably rely on a stable group of salespeople who had spent considerable time in the company, worked out of the same location, learned from their peers, and absorbed the selling organization culture.

Today's selling organization is a matrix of people from a broad variety of professional, corporate, and cultural backgrounds. They seldom work in the same location and are dispatched to the service or sales situation of the moment.

Marketplace Dynamics

Dig a Deeper Hole or Redirect Efforts?

Most of our clients, well aware of these selling environment changes, sincerely want to improve their selling organization to provide substantially better results for their customers. The primary issue for them is selecting what to do to achieve these improvements. Non-selection will result in initiative overload and will auger the selling organization into a deeper hole.

Some selling organizations continue to respond to these changes with practices which used to work in the past, but do not suit today's circumstances. These old-style actions have little effect on results in an environment so fluid, so competitive, and so complex. Here are some examples.

- Enroll some channel partners—next week

- Hire more people

- Reorganize the chairs on the Titanic—again

- Reduce expenses across the board

- Lean on our top 10 percent of the sales force (or customers) to save us again this year

- Lower the price to sell business that makes this quarter's plan or saves a customer
- Spend $500,000 to bring in one of the Big Few consulting companies to analyze the situation so we can tell the board we are taking action
- Send everyone through a class and hope it works—quickly
- Cancel all training, travel, and marketing until next quarter
- Put a new spin on tired products
- Change the commission plan
- Change out the people

These quick-fix initiatives do not work, or work only briefly. Quick fixes never meaningfully improve selling organization performance for two key reasons.

1. Sales leaders eventually burn out because they are not acting systematically. It takes too much energy to constantly patch problems that seem to crop up randomly. It takes even more energy to do it again and again. The patches fail to address the underlying problems.

2. Quick fixes are never leveraged. The selling organization is rarely enrolled and enthusiastic. In fact, a quick fix usually confirms a skeptical sales organization's disdain for headquarters' competency.

A sales manager of a new CPS client related the following situation to us, which illustrates the quick-fix syndrome.

> A few years ago, we had a few products, a defined sales cycle, and everyone knew what their job was. Marketing and salespeople created leads, which the salespeople drove through steps that culminated in an order. The products and services were delivered through our post-sales organization, and customer service handled most of the issues. Life was good. We were successful.
>
> Now, through acquisition and expansion of our product lines, we have an incredibly complex set of offerings that we can bring to the customer. But everyone seems to be spending most of their time on internally focused company initiatives, or responding to customer service issues or tactical competitive pressures. While there are pockets of success, it is not repeatable. These great acquisitions were squandered.

There is a better way. Enlightened sales executives remind themselves that the mission of their company is to make customers more successful, not tweak their organization for a short-term gain in results. The following valuable exercise begins to frame the answer. Picture the chaos we described earlier and this creative approach.

A CSO assembles a small group of thought leaders in her company. She asks them to put themselves in the shoes of their five most important customers' executive teams. Next, she asks six simple questions.

1. What would these executives say is the most valuable thing we do for them?

2. What would these executives say is the measurable value our company brings them?

3. What would they say we do to manage this relationship?

4. Would these executives ask our selling organization to work with them to develop and execute business-critical projects? Who would they invite?

5. What is different about what we do for them versus our competitors?

6. What would this customer volunteer as the most creative, powerful thing we could do to help them be successful?

Then she asks the million-dollar question, "Team, what is the short list of business-critical initiatives we must undertake to exceed the expectations of these five customers?"

Chapter Summary

The selling environment has dramatically changed over the last decade. Salespeople must contend with complex sales offerings and complicated client organizations. Distracting work demands grow in pace, volume, and complexity. Pulled in many directions, salespeople become strategically confused, reacting to both internal and external pressures rather than acting toward long-term goals.

The voice of the customer is critical to keep sales professionals grounded. At every turn, they must ask themselves, "Where can I extract value for my customer?"

2

Develop a Sales Agenda for Growth

If you don't have a plan, someone will make up one for you.

—*Jack Welch*

Sales leaders have always wrestled with the challenge, "How do I continuously evolve the sales function to deliver better results?" The underlying question is, "What are the critical pieces I must address in order to do that?"

The realities of our current business climate add a layer of complexity to a sales leader's dilemma. The relentless performance demands from customers, stockholders, and analysts in today's marketplace require that sales management be equally focused on delivering quarterly results and preparing for unforeseen economic or market downturns. As a result, a sales leader must look beyond current issues and anticipate how best to prepare the selling organization for sustainable results. As CPS partner, Ken Evans, says, "Sales leaders who do not create an agenda for success under both positive and negative marketplace scenarios are doomed to be at the mercy of others' decisions. Relying only on market upturns is a recipe for disaster."

What Is a Selling Organization Agenda?

For most people, an agenda means things to be done. A meeting agenda, for example, itemizes issues to address at a meeting. For a sales organization, a sales agenda identifies those factors that can seriously affect sales results, positively or negatively, singly or in combination. It represents a list of factors that sales leaders must take into consideration in the planning and conduct of selling organization activities. Our experience demonstrates that success in today's environment is a function of developing an agenda that hones the organization into a value-delivery machine.

Whatever the circumstances, sales leaders are ultimately accountable for the results of the selling organization. We have witnessed many sales leaders who choose to undertake an endless stream of tactical sales initiatives that are not linked to their companies' strategic objectives. Without a high-altitude view of all the factors to consider and address, it is not surprising that some initiatives produce friction within the company, with selling channels, or with customers. Unfortunately, when such friction occurs, a tired solution to the problem is to simply reorganize, creating even more chaos and inertia. Our research underscores that successful sales leaders understand that all functions impacting the selling organization must be addressed holistically. These leaders understand the interdependency of key functions and judiciously select the few things that have the greatest potential to drive sustained performance, accountability, and results.

The Sales Agenda as a Growth Strategy

There is no shortage of great ideas in which to invest time, talent, and money. Selection, funding, and implementation are challenges that require not only the personal commitment of the CSO, but the buy-in and active support of senior executives, middle managers, and line personnel in order to provide desired results. While the CSO does have the benefit of positional influence, we recognize that there is a wide range of stakeholder and market factors that must be considered, coordinated, and managed. Successful sales executives understand that their agenda, whatever shape it takes, must align tightly with the company's core strategy and address the requirements of key internal and external stakeholders. The selling organization can have an incredible impact on each stakeholder's short- and long-range goals only if the sales agenda is at the same time customer-focused, innovation-driven, and practical.

Customer-focused. The implicit power of a sales agenda is that it focuses the thinking, planning, and actions of the selling organization on the customer. The sales agenda becomes the *voice of the customer* because every initiative that the selling organization pursues is driven by an effort to serve customer needs and uncover ways to create additional value for the customer.

We recommend that the tenet, "Always start with the customer," become the guiding principle and foundation for the agenda.

Innovation-driven. An agenda that is customer-focused naturally leads to innovation. As the selling organization constantly seeks ways to create and deliver value to the customer, it improves its own performance, both internally and in relation to the customer. Innovation can move the selling organization toward differentiation and competitive advantage.

Practical sales leaders can only step up to the innovation plate when they have a good handle on their current circumstances. Leadership can only think outside the box when they understand fully and deeply what is actually going on today.

No matter how well things appear to be going, the selling organization always needs to be receptive to better methods, better targets, more efficiencies, and new opportunities. The sales agenda drives sales leaders and selling organizations to innovate—to make improvements to strategies, processes, and technologies, which means changes to the way people work.

We believe that a sales agenda is an invaluable strategic tool for selling organizations. In fact, the agenda forms the basis of our discussion of related issues throughout the book. Let's explore a model for an agenda that comprises what we believe are critical bases for selling organizations to cover to progress to high-performance selling.

An Agenda Model: The Research

At CPS, we wanted to test and confirm our belief that a sales agenda provides a solid basis for sustainable sales success, and to better understand the key issues affecting high-level sales executives, especially their priorities and initiatives to support customer-facing teams on strategic accounts.

To validate our hypothesis that a sales agenda facilitates sustainable growth, we initiated a research project in collaboration with one of our valued partners. On our behalf, Filigree Consulting, Inc. interviewed respondents with various responsibilities ranging from chief sales executives to divisional sales executives, with assigned business targets in the $200-million to $2-billion range. Respondents, many of whom had additional operational or marketing responsibilities, represented relationship-intensive industries, including high technology, durable goods distribution, and professional services companies.

To better understand the importance of having a documented sales agenda, we asked questions that helped us get a sense of the respondents' organization, planning constructs, role in the organization, organizational development, and critical success factors. Respondents were also invited to comment on the following sales agenda model we developed.

Chief Sales Officer Agenda Model

© 2002 by Critical Path Strategies, Inc. All Rights Reserved.

The model provides a high-level framework for describing, prioritizing, and communicating sales executive responsibilities and key priorities. In essence, the chief sales officer agenda model represents a super-set of issues sales leaders must purposefully address to ensure optimal selling organization performance.

The CSO agenda framework is in the shape of a pyramid to denote progressively more sales execution-oriented initiatives, starting from a foundation of corporate strategy to deployment, development, support, and finally, to delivering client value through account management execution. As our interviews progressed, we were not surprised by the wide range of approaches being used by respondents in delivering value, developing people resources, and focusing on customers.

Interestingly, all respondents concurred that having a framework to outline the critical functions of any successful sales organization enabled development of a more meaningful and comprehensive selling organization strategy. As one participant said, "The model provides peer-group alignment and a road map for the future." The model is useful not only for the sales organization, but for a range of functions in the company that interface with the sales organization.

Stop and think about the stakeholders who might impact—or be impacted by—your team's performance. Here is a partial list of key stakeholders.

Selling organization members. When selling organization members have a clear picture of issues that can have serious impacts on sales results, they are more likely to understand how those issues affect others in the agenda, and how their work fits into the bigger picture. With direction, sales leaders can apply more consistent and targeted actions to their daily work responsibilities.

C-level executives. Having a visual representation of what is required for successful account management execution can also be useful to a CEO, CFO, COO, and CIO. The model summarizes elements each C-level officer needs to consider in making particular decisions that can impact sales objectives or sales operations.

Non-sales functional leaders. Non-sales functional leaders may not be aware of how far-ranging sales activities can be. Policies and practices within non-sales areas can significantly impact what the sales organization is trying to achieve. An agenda model can help leaders in multiple areas to see the diverse but related activities needed for successful sales management.

We believe that all selling organizations must address each element included in the CSO agenda—at some point and in some way—to be successful over time. What becomes critically important is identifying, selecting, and prioritizing the few elements that have the greatest possibility of providing the desired business impact. The most successful sales leaders consider company culture, maturity of their management team, and ability of their organization to absorb and accept significant change in selecting two or three agenda elements on which to focus resources. There is no magic answer to the selection question except acknowledging that *you cannot do it all—all at once.* The top three priorities for one selling organization may be vastly different from those selected by another. Size of team, type of customer, go-to-market strategy, history of the company, and maturity of the industry can all affect the selection discussion.

Suffice it to say that careful consideration must be given to the process of identifying and choosing your organization's priorities. Review the following definitions of the CSO agenda blocks and think about what gaps might exist in your organization. Think about the linkages between your selling function and other integral parts of the company. Ask yourself and your team what improved results could occur from a renewed commitment to building a customer value-driven organization. Then, begin your journey.

Level 1: Developing a Coverage Strategy

Competition	Customer Segmentation	Value Recognition	Branding	Channels and Organization

The bottom level of the pyramid model provides the foundation for the selling organization that will support the complex requirements of its work. Like the foundation for a large building, a strategy for how the selling organization will undertake its activities needs to be solid and resilient, able to withstand changes in customer preferences, product lines, and economic conditions.

Establishing a good coverage strategy takes shape from aligning the elements of this level of the model into a coherent, customer-facing direction based on value for the customer and the company. It forms the basis for the selling organization's success and momentum.

Competition. Assessing the competitive landscape and go-to-market strategy is fundamental. You can boil the ocean with competitive analysis or just look at a few important competitors. One of our clients huddled together some bright sales managers and formed a "red team." The red team's mission was to formulate a strategy to improve their position—from a competitor's point of view.

- What is the competition doing?
- How do their offerings compare with ours?
- What adjustments need to be made to surpass them or find a unique direction or niche?
- What does SWOT analysis (strengths, weaknesses, opportunities, threats) indicate about comparative performance to rivals or win/loss rates and market share?

Customer segmentation. When sales leaders determine how they are going to position their company relative to the competition, they need to identify their target customer segments.

- What are logical segments based on some selection criteria? Are they all worth pursuing?
- Which groups are most profitable, most receptive to company offerings, or have the greatest potential for growth?
- How do these groups like to be served?

- How might the selling organization accommodate those needs?
- What groups will the selling organization target and with what resources?

Value recognition. If any of these foundation elements could be considered the most important, our vote would go to the box in the middle—value recognition. We define value recognition as the following.

- The value that a seller identifies as being important to the customer's needs and success (packaged in an offering, value proposition, and differentiators)
- The value that a buyer acknowledges in the seller's offering, way of doing business, and value delivery
- The actions and packaging that will allow a seller to win—even at a higher price

Branding. It is important to check the alignment of our selling strategy with our customer's branding strategy.

- What does our company stand for, and is that mission and value proposition consistent with our definition of value recognition?
- Is the customer getting the same message, the same look and feel, and the same experience from our company at all touch points?
- What process is used to ensure that sales collateral—including proposals and presentations—conforms to and supports the corporate image?

Channels and organization. The process of determining how best to deploy resources to support a customer's go-to-market strategy and associated segmentation drives the appropriate channels for distribution of the product or service. Sales leaders must develop coverage strategy to align with each distribution method to ensure that conflict is minimized. Some of our clients call this their routes-to-market plan.

Level 2. Deploying the Selling Organization

Hiring and Recruiting	Career Path	Compensation and Recognition	Sales Management and Leadership

This level of the pyramid is about setting the stage—putting in place the people and practices the selling organization will require to do outstanding work. Here, sales leaders establish how the selling organization will operate.

They declare the rules of the game, and establish fair policies and practices that demonstrate respect for the players and their contributions.

Hiring and recruiting. Responsible sales leaders want to recruit people with attitudes and skills that best represent their customer-facing organization. Also, to the extent possible, they want to put these people in positions that best align with their abilities and strengths. As author Jim Collins *(Built to Last: Successful Habits of Visionary Companies)* said, "You want not just the right people on the bus; you also want them in the right seats on the bus."

Most sales leaders do not have the luxury of installing a whole sales team of their choosing, and even then, their choices may not turn out to be what they expected. The chief executive officer of one of our long-time clients advises, "You have to take the hand you are dealt—the people you have—and work with it while constantly refreshing that hand of cards."

- What is the role model we should hire to?
- How can we best attract this kind of talent?
- What is an effective hiring process?
- Do we have a disciplined, quality-hiring program?
- How do we bring a new employee into our culture quickly?

Career path. Most good sales organizations want to keep their best resources close to customers. They need their best people to manage their best customer accounts and track and close on their best sales opportunities. In turn, these top resources want to increase their own human capital and make themselves more valuable to their profession, employer, and industry. They want and deserve a clear career path along which they can continuously demonstrate their value to the company and increase their own professional capital.

The company must provide opportunities that will both attract good candidates and keep good performers, as well as provide an incremental growth path for all salespeople to stretch and develop their abilities. Nobody will feel engaged in the job, or go the extra mile, if there are no milestones or horizons to reach.

As Harvard Business School professor, Rosabeth Moss Kanter, so succinctly put it, "People, people, people. Ask any future-oriented employer today what their biggest asset is, and that is their answer. Ask those same employers what their biggest headache is, and that is still the answer. Attracting people, motivating people, and retaining people."

Kanter's own answer to the issue is to seek the renewable commitment of employees by providing constantly updated value—for the employee. An attractive career path, linked to growing competence and increasing compensation, is a way to provide constantly updated value.

- How do we align our greatest talent with our greatest opportunities?
- What are critical skills and results that we should reward?
- How do we communicate expectations for advancement?

Compensation and recognition. By now, most sales and non-sales leaders are aware of the profound connection between rewards and results among their employees. The achievements leaders expect must be tied to the rewards they are prepared to offer. However, nearly everyone has a story about a damaging disconnect between what people were expected to accomplish and how differently they were rewarded.

- What is affordable funding for our compensation model?
- What compensation model is easiest to communicate and implement?
- What are our expectations for various levels of performance and the commensurate reward levels?
- Are they aligned with corporate objectives?
- Does this model drive and reward extraordinary performance?
- What formal and informal recognition programs might also motivate our teams toward extraordinary performance?

Compensation. Compensation is not the only way to keep or reward good people, but sales leaders need to be sure that their compensation plan is at least competitive with industry practices for the caliber of people they want to keep or acquire. The selling organization's practices for recognizing notable performance are motivators for the sales staff to achieve progressively more exceptional performance.

One of our colleagues described the fiercely competitive but secretive compensation practices in the company where he worked. Payment plans were ambiguous and discretionary. Despite being overpaid for their efforts compared to the industry, the sales staff felt cheated and kept in the dark. The plan did not have positive performance effects.

It is no surprise that people's behavior changes in response to expectations and rewards in the compensation plan. A clear compensation plan is a way to recognize top performers and to highlight their achievements for others to follow.

Recognition. "A pat on the back and recognition of a job well done goes further than most people think," observes CPS partner, Mary Ann Costello, who was once responsible for designing and managing the IBM sales compensation plan. She asserts people will go the extra mile when leaders show salespeople they care about individual performance.

Of course, everyone likes to be recognized for achievements—for their individual competence and contribution to a larger whole. This is particularly true for sales professionals who are generally achievement-oriented. They appreciate recognition for their efforts from the sales organization and peers, certainly, but especially from customers who they have served well.

Public recognition of salespeople's efforts within the selling organization has trophy value. There are two important effects of such recognition.

1. Recipients will be spurred to further excellence by having their competence and contribution validated among their peers.

2. Their example can be a role model for others who seek to validate their own work: *She must be doing something right. I'd better find out what that is.*

In this way, sales leaders can move the performance of the group's collective efforts forward another notch toward excellence.

Sales management and leadership. Without enlightened sales leadership and good sales management, there is little likelihood of a sales organization acting in a consistent way to deliver regular, reliable results.

Sales leadership sets the bar for outstanding behavior and extraordinary goals, constantly motivating, coaching, supporting, and strengthening the sales team. Sales management, at all levels, must make the right things happen at the right time in the right way. What happens on the front lines shows up on the bottom line.

- How do we align our sales management team with the strategy?
- How do we help them align the company's needs with the needs of their selling teams?
- How do we equip them to be coaches?
- How do we build their enthusiasm for making a difference into a contagious passion for the business?

Level 3. Developing the Selling Organization

Skills Development	Measurement	Pipeline Management

The agenda model acknowledges the need for advancing competencies in the sales organization and taking actions that allow those competencies to flourish. In other words, not developing skill levels and talents of the sales force would be like drafting a baseball team and never practicing.

Measurement enables the firm to track individual and collective performance—not just revenue results. Pipeline management is the critical tool that helps us understand the viability of each territory and our collective view of the future based on the fruits of our labor today.

Skills development. Sales leaders usually have an uneven set of skilled performers. They need to give their performers every kind of support to perform better, and that includes clear directions and expectations, assessment of performance, and suitable rewards and recognition. It also must include opportunities for skill development and strengthening of competencies. Because things change, new challenges arise, and new abilities are required to meet them, leaders also need to keep the field fresh for their players, to give them new ways to stretch and excel so they can enlarge their own personal capital.

Sales leaders must determine what set of skills the sales force needs to be successful, and then provide the means for people to develop them. Both groups benefit handsomely from doing so. Salespeople gain confidence when they enhance their own competence, and have a sense of mastery over their domain of activity. They make better judgments and engage more fully in their work. They become what leaders want: *a capable, confident, high-performance sales team.*

- What is a basic skills profile for a successful sales career?
- What are current skill levels and gaps?
- What training investment are we willing to make?
  - One time? Sustained?
- What are the critical skill gaps and how can we best fill them?

Measurement. Performance measurement gets a bad rap in most quarters. Some people dismiss it as irrelevant; some find it unfair; others fear it for exposing either small imperfections, or in some cases, giant lies. Poor measurement is at the core of many problems in sales organization effectiveness.

A badly designed measurement system can cause dysfunctional behavior. Performance measurement is intended to give an equitable reading of progress, identify problems and correct them, and reward excellence. Instead, it often becomes an exercise so counterproductive and wasteful that it warrants monitoring itself. The bigger problem is that in some sales organizations, no measurement is undertaken at all, and excuses are easy to find.

- It is too complicated.
- It is too much trouble.
- The IT systems are not up to the job.
- We get updates at regular meetings.
- Financials will tell us what we need.

In others, the measurement of sales progress is perfunctory at best, irrelevant at worst. Failing to track sales progress and performance will lead the selling organization downward at an accelerating pace. Everyone has heard that what you measure is what you get. The sales leader's challenge is to measure what matters.

Pipeline management. Pipeline management is at the core of all sales activity because, fundamentally, the value of the pipeline is the value of the business. Selling organizations have the mandate to drive pipeline volume, quality, and velocity. Managing the pipeline is essentially the selling organization's job. It is fundamental in monitoring progress and highlighting looming problems.

Pipeline Management Fundamentals

Establish best practices for selling stages, mapped to customer outcomes	→	
Map activities to move from stage to stage: • Establish technical fit • Identify relationship actions • Demonstrate utility and value to the customer • Implement strategy to create value and urgency • Enroll the team to execute	→	**Predictable** **Sustainable** **Results**
Coach to success	→	
Measure velocity, quality, and quantity	→	

In our view, a well-designed and well-managed sales process is essential for driving this critical aspect of the sales agenda. Later chapters look at how other key features of successful sales organizations contribute to successful pipeline management.

Level 4: Supporting the Selling Organization

Sales and Marketing Support	Customer Service

Even if a selling organization has the first three levels of the sales agenda covered, there will be ongoing challenges. Resources will be stretched, problems will certainly surface, energies may dissipate, and those goals that energized everybody at the outset start to look far off in the distance indeed.

Sales success and customer loyalty are usually the result of a company's ability to deliver on its promises. This ability typically falls short in two moments of truth.

1. The sales team's responsiveness to a customer need with the right solution at the right time

2. The customer service team's ability to handle an inquiry or complaint

All sales forces—even the best—need to be supported by important complementary functions. They all need front-facing support from marketing, and the rear-guard actions of customer service. Marketing messaging and customer service can wrap the sales function in a supportive, mutually beneficial environment from which sales can marshal its best energies for its best opportunities.

Sales and marketing support. Some marketing departments and sales departments work well together. Sales benefits from advice and support from marketing, which in turn sees its messages translated into closed transactions by sales. Unfortunately, this is not often the case.

In our view, it should not be difficult for sales and marketing groups to work well together. They are both working toward the same end: creating and selling company offerings. Their common goal is to provide extraordinary value in a way that the customer recognizes it and that realizes exceptional value for the company.

If each group is shooting for the same target, then each can provide the best advice and expertise to the other, and welcome that help from a respected source. Marketing and sales can work from the same value messages, address the same value points, work toward implementation of solutions that bring value to the customer, and engage in long-term growth and maintenance of relationships.

The marketing group can ask the sales group the same question that sales asks of the customer, "What can I do for you today?" The sales group needs to alert marketing to difficulties in the field, and specify the help they need.

Customer service. Customer service is the ultimate test of value for a company's offering, which must be delivered on time, on budget, and implemented well. Any problems must be promptly fixed. If customer service is poor, the selling effort becomes rapidly undervalued.

Unresponsiveness to customers usually results in poor retention rates. A herd of new customers brought into the fold counts little if they leave just as surely en masse. That means that revenue gains are washed out and profitability lines are hammered—going up the down escalator again.

When something goes wrong, the event is a moment of truth for the seller to manage to the customer's satisfaction. If problems are resolved and confirmed to ensure that the customer is satisfied, and if this is done well, the company gains additional credit for its reliability, and an extra measure of customer loyalty. *They did what they said they would do.*

Level 5. Delivering Client Value

> Account Management
> Execution

Although every part of the sales agenda implies the delivery of client value, this top level of the pyramid focuses on the ultimate goal of all sales activities: *good account management execution.* In our research with 25 sales executives, every one of them listed this as one of their top three initiatives. This is where the rubber meets the road, where selling professionals are eye-to-eye with customers. This is the final and most important step in delivering client value—developing and executing on customer plans.

Account management execution has several component activities similar to the CSO agenda model. Like the CSO agenda model, these component activities are all required in various combinations to produce the best results. This subset of activities is based on the assumption that a solid business-to-business strategy at the account level produces the greatest breakthrough results for both buyer and seller. The account management execution model will be fully explored later in the book.

The Agenda as the Customer's Voice

It is particularly important to make sure that sales agenda directions, especially the top initiatives, are firmly tied to customer benefits. Under the leadership of enlightened sales leaders, the agenda becomes the *voice of the customer* for the selling organization.

The sales agenda can be used as a template for focusing the many aspects of sales organization activities on the needs of customers and potential value offerings to customers. For every element of the agenda, especially the three or four key initiatives selected, the selling organization needs to critically evaluate how these initiatives *advance the interests of the customer.*

One of those selected initiatives, for example, might be sustained attention to sales team development. If the design point is only to close deals faster, it misses the mark. If the design point is to sustainably serve customers, it is on target. Another initiative might address the hiring model—what kind of people do customers want to deal with?

Sales organizations that hear the voice of the customer can reap the following big benefits.

Focused and energized salespeople. When salespeople's attention is never far from customer interests, they work more effectively and, because their efforts are concentrated, with more energy.

Simplified work of sales leaders. When all elements of the agenda are connected to the interests of customers, the complexity of a sales leader's work is reduced because all lines lead to the customer.

Consistent actions in selling organization. When agenda items are aligned with customer issues, there is less diffusion of effort.

The Other Customer

Extraordinary sales organizations focus on other customers too—these being the other functional areas of the business. The goal here is to understand their needs and pains, get them enrolled, and work as a team in executing the agenda. These other customers can include groups such as research and development, channels, marketing, customer service, consulting, finance, and outside strategic suppliers.

That is not to say that agenda items should not benefit the sales organization. Of course they should. If the fundamental premise for the business is to profitably serve customers, all constituencies must be customer-focused.

The whole point of all sales activity is to serve customers well, to create value for them and the selling company. The sales agenda is a good place to start with customers, and make them the focus of all targeted actions.

Chapter Summary

The chief sales officer agenda lays out the key issues affecting high-level sales executives, with a specific focus on how they manage and support their key customer-facing teams.

The agenda is modeled around five major levels of selling organization support: developing a coverage strategy, deploying the selling organization, developing the selling organization, supporting the selling organization, and delivering client value. The agenda provides a framework to help executives surface issues and identify the most critical areas for improvement within their organizations to bring additional value. It helps focus resources and selling organization efforts on what matters. The voice of the customer provides the acid test in evaluating sales organization activities.

3

Activate the Sales Agenda

The secret of success is constancy to purpose.

—*Benjamin Disraeli*

For sales leaders, there is always too much to do, unanticipated issues rear up to cause problems, and people go off in different directions to meet their obligations. They might think, "How do I get the time to put all these responsibilities into some kind of coherent order—even if it would stay that way for only a minute? Anyway, I have to trust my people to do the right things; they are professionals."

The first challenge in working with the sales agenda, as outlined in the model, is finding the time to address its components. There is only a limited amount of resources sales leaders can access and leverage at any one time, and a limited number of things they can do in a particular time period. The sales force, too, has a finite amount of energy to be expended over their universe of opportunities. The sales agenda model gives sales leaders a view of the elements they must consider for selling organization management, but they cannot move on all fronts at once.

Secondly, sales leaders cannot successfully move on even a few fronts without the support of company executives, on the one hand, and of the front-line salespeople on the other. Company executives can be instrumental in providing resources from their areas of responsibility to help the selling organization achieve its sales agenda objectives. The commitment of salespeople, and of important non-salespeople, is obviously necessary to making the agenda work well.

For the first challenge, we recommend that sales leaders focus their energy on selecting priorities and turning them into projects. For the second, we strongly advise sales leaders to enlist support of executives across the company to ensure that the entire selling organization and key non-sales colleagues understand and support the priorities and are committed to driving them forward.

Select Short-Term Priorities

When sales leaders decide to work with a sales agenda, they do not expect the selling organization to stop doing business and focus solely on rebuilding selling teams on a different foundation. To some, that would be like changing the tires on a car while it is moving at 80 miles per hour down the highway. They need to address the following tough issues.

- Where should I spend (what proportion of) my team's time and resources?
- How much change can my organization withstand, and over what time period?
- How do I get everything done that has to be done, and make sure that we make progress on the important fronts?

Essentially, sales leaders need to decide what critical initiatives will debilitate the selling organization if they are not implemented. These become the selling organization's *year one sales agenda*. Other critical initiatives can be pursued at the same time with reduced attention, or more fully in a subsequent year.

We recommend that leaders choose a limited number of priorities to address. There should be no more than three or four key initiatives to work on at one time, usually over a year. One hot item, for example, could be strengthening teams; another could focus on improving channels effectiveness, or perhaps building a sales pipeline review process. These hot items are in addition to regular sales activities, but they are all practical ways to improve selling organization performance, driven by one key metric.

Within the sales agenda model, sales leaders can address issues that are most important to their strategy and operations. They can direct activities within these areas according to their organization's goals and priorities—at various levels of intensity and at various times. We recommend two simple criteria for selecting the key areas of focus.

- **Reward**. What are the reward factors for each of the potential initiatives?
- **Ability to execute**. How difficult will it be to undertake each initiative?

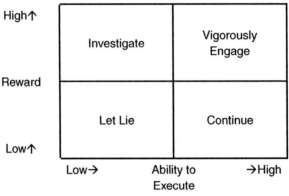

Short-Term Priorities Matrix

For example, sales leaders may consider it extremely important to introduce a measurement system for sales activities, but the information systems in the company are not up to the task, and are undergoing major renovation over the next year. This project will need to wait.

Sales leaders need to do some spadework to determine the best places to focus selling organization priorities and energies. A good place to start is to ask the selling organization's most important clients about how value is being provided by the extended selling team. This can be very revealing, if somewhat unsettling. Secondly, put yourself in the shoes of your competitors. Do a SWOT analysis from their perspective.

A third resource is to ask some of the company's best and brightest. Collectively, they can evaluate potential initiatives to come up with a short list of the most urgent and critical initiatives the selling organization should undertake. This is a rigorous approach that will go a long way toward extracting commitment. Here are some steps we recommend.

Assess Selling Organization Status/Strength

First, sales leaders must determine the elements in the sales agenda model that are most important. They explore what the company's offerings should be to be significantly more successful in the marketplace. This is an outward-looking exercise. What would make the most difference for the selling organization? What would generate the greatest returns? This is not just a wish list. It is a reasonable match between potential results and focused action in certain areas of the sales agenda.

Then they can rank these items according to their potential positive impact on sales success. Some agenda initiatives might present a clear route to great rewards, whereas the potential for others to return value may not be so evident. This exercise gives sales leaders a picture of which actions can bring the greatest benefit in their market circumstances. This discipline begins to develop the comparative value of each possible initiative to the company.

Determine Current Status/Future Possibilities

Next, assess where the selling organization stands in relation to these ranked areas of focused attention. Here are some questions to ask.

- Are there serious shortcomings in a particular agenda area?
- How far away is the selling organization currently from a performance level in a certain area that could make a big difference?
- What kind of resource commitment would be required to get to a level that would produce results?
- How executable is the initiative?

Then, sales leaders and key participants need to determine what the selling organization could realistically achieve in the short-term, in light of their current status and available resources. Following are some typical questions that might be posed.

- What is the political climate for a certain course of action?
- What level of achievement is realistically possible?
- Who else in the company should participate to make it a reality?
- Are there champions in the executive ranks or top performers among the sales force who could help advance the initiative?

All of this analysis will help to narrow the potential areas of focus and further clarify the return on investment of effort.

Select Priorities with the Biggest Returns

Finally, sales leaders need to choose the initiatives that are most important to meet selling organization objectives and most doable. They need results, remember, and there is little point in setting a goal that the group cannot reach, or reach only with disproportionate effort. The initiatives chosen should, at minimum, address the following two areas.

1. Provide the *biggest bang for the buck*

2. Act as a magnet for best practices and behaviors that sales leaders want to instill in the selling organization

Sales leaders will need to spend most of their time and resources on these initiatives, but it is these initiatives that will generate the greatest benefit.

Working on these priorities may have positive effects on other parts of the company's organization that sales leaders may not have anticipated. Also, when a selling organization is trying to introduce change to improve its performance, the agenda provides a basis for *what needs to change*, and *how*, and even *when* relative to what else is going on in the rest of the company.

A plan is just a dream without targeted actions, however, and an action plan is just a list without schedules and accountabilities. The priorities or hot spots need to be managed like projects or they will fade into the dust of daily hassles.

> One of our clients, a chief sales officer for a software and services support firm focused primarily on the insurance industry, needed to reevaluate the effectiveness of his sales organization. The organization model and processes had served the firm well for several years, and they had developed an admirable growth record for a small company. Success led them to realize that they could do much more for their current clients, and for the many new opportunities identified on the horizon. However, the sales organization was stretched.
>
> Because of his intuitive sales leadership style, the CSO had been able to be engaged in every deal, but he was discovering that his personal effectiveness was dissipating. It seemed that every deal was in crisis. His salespeople were chasing some bad deals. Some of his top performers were leaving. His board of directors and CEO desperately wanted to grow, but the sales engine was not responding. The pipeline was not predictable. They lost some deals they believe they should have won. His calendar and the calendars of his sales and sales support teams were a wreck. Something had to change.
>
> CPS worked with the CSO to determine the future state of the business, what the business could look like. Correspondingly, we helped design the future state of the sales organization. Using the CSO agenda framework, we developed a road map built on planning, process, and execution initiatives to lead the sales and support teams to success. In 12 months time, the sales teams exceeded their commitments, and the pipeline supported the business plan. The key was to identify and

address the most important gaps in the organization to reclaim, and leverage, its selling effectiveness. In this case, the critical elements for year one were market segmentation, pipeline management, and account management execution.

Establish Key Initiatives as Projects

The top three initiatives identified by sales leaders now need engines to keep momentum. These projects for improving the sales organization deserve full project management efforts. There are several steps to take to ensure the initiatives move forward.

Appoint project sponsors and project managers. The first thing to do is to appoint project managers for each key initiative. These need to be people who carry considerable authority and respect. They are considered the go-to people throughout the company. Sales leaders need access to them because they control resources that can bring the initiatives into focus quickly. Following are some of the typical criteria for selection.

- Critical thinker
- Solid project management skills
- Incisive listener
- Strong communications skills
- Thorough, but disciplined, analysis

Many of our clients turn these into Six Sigma projects and assign a black belt as project manager.

Establish project teams. Sales leaders need to establish project teams and populate them with smart people, but not just from sales or a functional area particularly related to the initiative. Participants should cover a representative range of functions across the enterprise, since the sales initiatives affect other parts of the organization, and should not be seen as self-serving for the sales group.

Typically, leaders would enlist people from the financial side of the business because the initiatives have financial implications. They would also benefit from participation of customer service, operations, and human resources representatives.

Develop project plans—the Critical Path. The project team then develops a project plan for the initiative—the pieces of work required to move this initiative forward. The plan must establish the scope of the project—what needs to be done by whom and by when—and focus on initiative-critical objectives first. What actions will yield the most value?

- Identify objectives
- Identify critical decisions to be made
- Identify major milestones to be accomplished
- Establish an appropriate timeline
- Assign appropriate responsibilities for each milestone
- Develop a communications plan for contacts and updates to the project plan

Sales leaders need to remember that they are working with people who already have day jobs. They do not have time for repetitive and inconclusive sessions on selected sales projects. Project managers must be cognizant of this reality and respect the team members by addressing the following items.

- Acknowledge their value as internal consultants to provide best thoughts and perspectives on this project
- Ask for solid recommendations within no more than 60 days with weekly checkpoints
- Facilitate the sessions; make it worthwhile for them to attend meetings that do not waste their time

It is important to set up a review process, which will enable sales leaders to make inevitable course corrections that are required. Reviews will further momentum by ensuring every part of the project is working at peak efficiency and effectiveness.

> The previously mentioned CSO asked CPS for another skull session on phase two of his sales organization's development. He and his team had been recognized for their success. He received a promotion with additional resources and responsibilities, including marketing and customer service. How could he best invest these resources to take the customer-facing organization to the next level? This time, selling skills, marketing programs, metrics, and customer service initiatives were selected as key differentiators. But here was his dilemma: How do we initiate and manage these projects on time and on budget while tending to our day jobs of selling and delighting customers? CPS helped the team develop a *dashboard* (or scorecard) that helped the extended sales, service, and support organization periodically and quickly review project status and areas in particular need of attention.

Project owners should also anticipate barriers, and identify those most likely to surface on the way to the project's objectives. These can include organizational and political barriers, as well as old reliable barriers to change. By anticipating these barriers, sales leaders may remove or lower some of these obstacles in the early stages of a project. The next challenge is to gain the support of executives across all lines of business.

Secure leadership support. To make progress on key sales agenda initiatives, sales leaders need to solicit agreement and support from company leadership. After all, initiatives undertaken by the sales group affect the entire company, as does their success, or lack of it.

Sales leaders usually need a great deal of diplomacy to deal with other organizational functions that can affect sales success. There are always issues of resource commitment. All company initiatives compete for senior executives' mind share and resources. With company leadership behind their efforts, sales leaders can make better progress in securing non-sales colleagues' support.

Even better, a clear rationale for key sales agenda initiatives helps to present selling organization objectives as cogent, well-developed plans for action, which can benefit a range of organizational functions.

> "I was so tired of being second-guessed by the COO, the CFO, the head of human resources, the general counsel, and other executives," a client CSO told us. When he presented his initiatives, or asked for their help, they were understandably skeptical, especially if the plans required some investment from them. They did not understand why these initiatives were important for the whole company, and not just self-serving actions on the part of the sales organization.
>
> Our client used a representation of the CSO agenda to illustrate to his colleagues why his initiatives were important, both for sales and the rest of them, how the company as a whole would benefit, what was already in place, what he was working on, what he needed help with, and what remained to be done.
>
> He even color-coded the stages of progress. People understood the situation easily. They could then ask specific questions. They could see how the pieces fit together, and how they could play a role. The CSO was able to explain, "Here is how we can get this done to maximize our sales investment!"

Develop a strong business case for top sales initiatives. Most non-sales executives have never worked in sales. They may be familiar with a strategy for capturing new markets, for new product development, or for efficiency improvements from information technology infrastructure upgrades, but not with a business case for improving the selling organization or for initiatives to boost sales growth.

The selling organization business case outlines what the selling organization intends to focus on, and why. Sales leaders must provide a set of compelling reasons for these actions and their expected outcomes. In addition, the CSO should review the high-level project plans and timelines.

The business case also outlines why these key initiatives are important for *everyone else* in the company. Smart sales leaders show how key sales initiatives can help colleagues *achieve their own business objectives.* This double-barreled business case increases the likelihood of support. Translating these projects into results per share is the ultimate.

A good business case builds confidence in sales leadership on the part of other key functional leaders in the company. They think, "These folks know what they are talking about, and they have provided some credible reasons for why they are going in that direction. I can see how it will help the company, and it can help my group, too. I will try to contribute from my end."

Invite leaders to help create strategy and action plans. One of the best ways to secure the support of company leadership for sales initiatives is to involve executives in the development of sales strategies, especially for important accounts. The important thing to get across is: *We are in this together.* Non-sales executives can be invited to work with sales strategy development teams, or asked to review strategies and provide suggestions.

The most effective sales agenda implementation occurs when sales leaders enroll cross-functional executives to participate on sales teams to develop specific account strategy and execution plans.

> One CPS client recruited 25 executives, each of whom served on the selling team as the executive sponsor for a selected customer for a minimum of three years. They participated actively in strategy reviews and accepted relationship-building assignments willingly. They called on selected customers quarterly to advance the strategy and monitor progress.
>
> In addition, and perhaps more importantly, these 25 executives became in tune with the voice of the customer, making the CSO's job of molding the company to a more market-driven organization much easier. Customer focus replaced internal focus.

Involve leaders in specific actions. When sales leaders face a situation where assistance from a subject-matter expert resource would be valuable, they can approach those executives who already understand the agenda and key initiatives to lend their influence. We recommend that sales leaders approach the executive in a way that creates energy and enthusiasm—with an *opportunity* that benefits the executive and the customer. There may be a problem associated with the situation, but it is the opportunity that gets the executive engaged.

A typical situation could be a sales team leader needing an executive to meet with a customer to convince the customer that the company can deliver what the team is proposing. We recommend that the sales team prepare a briefing sheet for the executive outlining the situation (here is where we are) and the opportunity (this is what we could achieve).

This package might include a call plan and set of suggested actions for the executive to take. It is important to be crisp with the executive's time. Schedule a time to debrief for best next actions.

Communicate the agenda. The sales agenda represents a new way of doing things—for salespeople, non-salespeople, and company executives and managers. It should be presented so that people understand it.

- What are we changing?
- Why are we changing?
- How will it work differently?
- Who is responsible for what?
- When will we implement this?

The key initiatives and project plans should be communicated clearly to sales teams and non-sales colleagues who can affect the outcomes of these initiatives. They need a map of the terrain and reason for the journey.

Launch the agenda. The launch of the agenda should be planned and managed with extreme care. In fact, it should be treated like a marketing campaign. Some of our clients even enroll a member of the company marketing team to develop the internal campaign.

> One of our clients invented a marketing tagline for the sales agenda launch. They called it *Urgency—Action—Excellence*. The agenda was quickly accepted and these three words captured the theme of the agenda's intent.

Launching the new sales agenda can be seen as similar to launching new products. Technology products, for example, that create value for the user are presented to the marketplace in a way that integrates the voice of the market and the voice of the technology provider. This involves analyzing, planning, and controlling customer-impacting resources, policies, and activities. Its purpose is to satisfy chosen customer groups' needs at a profit.

In a similar vein, the CSO is launching something new. Just as the launch of a new technology product is grounded in the wants and needs of chosen customer groups, the launch of the sales agenda should be grounded in the needs of the company as it supports customers.

The CSO has to carefully assess the characteristics of the groups to be impacted, and determine their preferred way of receiving communication. There are many questions to consider.

- What are the employee constituent groups to be targeted?
- What are their roles and client responsibilities?
- Who are the team members?
- Are there channel groups or suppliers who will be affected?
- What is their role in supporting the agenda?
- What message needs to be conveyed?
- How should the message be delivered to each group?
- What type of reinforcement is necessary?
- What deliverables should be provided?

At every level, sales leaders have an obligation to make it clear to their team what will be involved in this effort, and what each person's responsibilities will be in relation to those priorities. Here are some more recommendations for sales leaders.

- Immerse the management team in the project first; make sure they understand their roles as coaches and process leaders
- Identify role models to become internal champions for the initiative; reward the role models; penalize the naysayers
- Be visible in leadership; model the behavior
- Seize every opportunity to talk about key initiatives in meetings and other company events
- Make sure that field teams understand the messages to be communicated to customers before trying to send the team to any training sessions
- Communicate the sales agenda to everyone—relentlessly

Now, the short-term agenda is ready for action. What actions will move these key initiatives forward with the most effectiveness and velocity? We recommend adopting a *critical path* methodology to balance the elements of what will be very important initiatives for enhancing the selling organization's abilities and sales results.

Taking the Critical Path

Effectively announcing the new agenda is one thing, but getting it completed is the dilemma. We recommend managing this as a project coupled with a plan—a *critical path plan*. It helps to answer the constantly recurring question, in any circumstance, "What are the critical things that will help me run this play faster and better?" It consists of critical actions to reach the goal or solve the problem—not any actions, but the highest-impact actions, the optimum route to the desired result.

Our critical path starts with the future—identifying selling organization priorities that would make the most difference to performance. It then works backward to develop a plan for how to get there with the best use of resources. Essentially, a critical path in the selling organization environment is a *business plan for sales results*.

Taking the necessary steps for working with the agenda, and putting the selling organization on a critical path for making anticipated progress, prepares sales leaders for one of their biggest challenges: *introducing change into everyday activities*.

Chapter Summary

From the full sales agenda, sales leaders select a limited number of priorities on which to work in the short term. These *hot spots* are the most important ways to improve key aspects of selling organization performance. These improvement initiatives deserve the attention of full project management efforts.

The CSO and sales leaders need agreement from the company's leadership on the initiatives that will have the greatest impact on sales results. They also need the solid support of their sales teams and non-sales colleagues to advance the sales agenda. All participants must understand the purpose of the initiatives and their role in them. Creating a critical path captures the actions to be taken according to a disciplined schedule to achieve the objectives of the project, including the best returns on resources invested.

PART 2.
BUILD A FOUNDATION FOR RESULTS

Experience tells us that meaningful progress toward changing the way an organization acts takes relentless focus on the right things at the right time. With a focused sales agenda and a set of key strategic initiatives, the selling organization's old ways of doing business must be supplemented with new behaviors. With change comes uncertainty for the people whose energy and dedication are most needed.

Although change creates an environment of risk for most people, properly initiated change provides everyone with excitement and opportunity. Scores of books have been written about change and change management; from this we can infer that few companies do it well. We see many recent examples, especially in the implementation of major business process software applications such as CRM, in which millions of dollars are spent on important and strategic initiatives that often fail to meet expectations. So what can be done to ensure success at each level of the organization?

When sales leaders are required to make changes to the selling organization, often as a result of items in the sales agenda, they are really looking at changing the way people think and behave. Everything they want to accomplish hinges on how they manage the people who will act on the new directions of the organization. The sales leader needs to focus on the day-to-day attitudes and actions of the people who make the selling organization succeed, the internal business processes, the effectiveness of the changes to achieve results, and the messages that customers receive from marketing and customer service to ensure consistency and clarity.

It takes much more than posting up strategic initiatives and developing new processes to change people's behaviors. It takes a deep understanding of how to help people find a new set of possibilities for themselves to transform an organization into believers and implementers that will produce extraordinary results. This section is about how sales leadership can mobilize change through the culture of the selling organization.

This section focuses on establishing a blueprint for successful change. It begins with acknowledging that a sales culture exists and is difficult to modify, but sales behavior must be changed in order to effect different results. Cultural change starts with leadership's commitment to change the culture's conversations from *us-focused* to *customer-focused*. We also have a brief discussion on segmentation and aligning the organization to the voice of the customer, and changing conversations from selling something to creating value. We will also explore some pragmatic organizational and process work we have observed clients undertake that enable selling organizations to more effectively align how they do business with customer environments.

4

Introduce Change

There is nothing more difficult to take in hand, more perilous to conduct, or more uncertain in its success, than to take the lead in the introduction of a new order of things.

—Niccolo Machiavelli, in The Prince (1532)

The Selling Organization Culture

A company's culture is embodied in its collective perceptions, perspectives, and value. It is the answer people on the team give to the question, "What is it like to work around here?" The culture takes shape around conversations about the way things are done and the judgments by which priorities are determined, and the quiet undercurrents that define those actions and beliefs as acceptable or unacceptable. In its simplest sense, culture is about conversations.

The way people speak, listen, think, and act are all manifestations of a cultural norm, a kind of company conversation. Within the larger organizational construct there can be sub-cultures of specialized functions or groups. Many people still regard the information technology group as a kind of alien species that has its own dialect. Some might see finance as concerned only with running the numbers. People have their own colorful views of salespeople as well.

What all these diverse perceptions amount to are filters of belief. Within these collective filters of belief are individual filters—all different, indicating various shades of confidence or insecurity, self-esteem, or fear. The dominant belief filters in an organization govern how people think, behave, act, and make choices.

For example, if senior management effectively signals a belief in profit by any means, others in the organization might adopt those beliefs collectively, and get to work on improving margins. Collective belief adopted from leaders, however, can be dispelled by contrary experience. As we stated earlier, new ideas need proof of experience. If employees discover that margin results are not rewarded, or if they do not suffer the consequences of not improving margins, they will not make the choices needed for the desired outcomes.

In general, people do what they believe to be right in ways that they believe will bring them the desired results as they perceive them. As Henry Ford said, "If you believe you can do a thing or not, you are right." In order to remain viable in the changing marketplace, the challenge for most sales leaders and the real need today is motivating the majority of the selling team to act like top performers (your role models).

Depart from the Status Quo

Efforts to change even some aspects of selling organization culture can be a difficult struggle as resistance to change is particularly more entrenched in selling teams. Why? Fragile egos, fear of loss of control, and the uncertainty of expectations. Sales leaders often will hear responses like, "The way things are is fine," or "This will never work," or "My customers will never go for it." Those old ways will envelop change efforts with a fine mist of resistance. The norm becomes synonymous with security—change is threatening.

Many people have worked in at least one organization in which the leadership fires up the troops with a lofty goal, "We are going to be 'over there' in a year!" Everyone says, "I want to be a part of it!" However, after the initial kick-off, only 10 percent of the people get on board; another 10 percent do nothing about it and never will; and the other 80 percent are open to change, but likely will not do so unless there are *intentional leadership actions that visibly reinforce that change.* Without this demonstrable mandate, the great plan dies, crushed by the relentless weight of inertia.

Most people, and salespeople in particular, prefer to be in their comfort zone. They deal with people they like and who like them, and they spend time on projects that fit their style and schedule. It is fine to rely on tried and true methods for solving problems and addressing customer needs. However, today's customer satisfaction issues may be different and require responses that are not as familiar to the sales organization. They will hesitate to implement without solid proof and a strong belief that, first, they personally will not be negatively impacted and, secondly, that these new responses will work and have been proven. Those 10 percent at the top of your sales organization that buy in will try, but it is the 80 percent that must be moved to change. The bottom 10 percent need to work elsewhere.

Change comes through efforts that push the envelope, or make people feel a little uncomfortable and uncertain. Growth, for individuals and organizations, is the process of challenging or updating people's belief filters. The first step is for people to accept that filters can be reconfigured—that there is another way to look at things. It also requires proof of experience—through feedback, reinforcement, and reward—which convinces people to alter their beliefs and act differently.

Most people base their behavior on what they understand (the plan for their actions) and on what they see (tangible results as a consequence of those actions). Confidence comes from successes, not just words or strategies. Taking on change is tough work, whether with a large account team, technical group, or the entire customer-facing team.

Change the Majority

One of our clients measured the contributions of their individual performers relative to the collective sales results of the company. They confirmed the 80-20 phenomenon, but in this case it was 80-10. Ten percent of their salespeople were leading teams producing 80 percent of the revenue. No sales organization that dreams of achieving extraordinary results can rely on only the top 10 percent of its sales performers for long.

Let's put the calculator to this. If a sales organization has 100 people and a bell curve of 10 percent top performers, 80 percent average performers, and 10 percent bottom performers, and you believe you can effectively leverage a five percent improvement from each, the following chart highlights the leverage.

Salespeople and Performance Level	Sales Revenue	Number of People	Percent Improvement	Yield
10% Top	$ 1.50M	10	5%	$ .75M
80% Average	$ .80M	80	5%	$ 3.20M
10% Bottom	$ .30M	10	5%	$ .15M

The $3.2 million jumps off the chart. The top 10 percent will probably get it anyway, and the bottom 10 percent is hardly worth the effort.

Leadership is motivating the 80 percent of the people in the middle of the sales organization to act in new ways to achieve desired outcomes. This group either carries an initiative along with the momentum of their commitment and energy, or drags it down to a crawl and eventual demise, with the weight of their indifference. Leaders who want successful outcomes need to drive best practices and actions to produce results in the collective behavior of the majority of the sales staff.

Here are some change initiatives that CPS has observed.

- Change the conversation to *customer-first*
- Align the organization to *customer-first*
- Validate *customer value* in the customer's language
- Set extraordinary goals to *drive extraordinary behavior*

Customer-First Conversations

"It is all about the customer," declared one of our CSO clients in a conversation with his sales managers. "What is?" they asked. "Everything," he replied.

One of the best ways to promote change in a selling organization is to change conversations people have with each other to better focus on the customer. Different conversations lead people to different ways of thinking. They can gravitate to different ways of behaving. Changing conversation changes both the focus and the way people think, which changes the way people behave.

Management must challenge the status quo through intentional focus and questions about old assumptions of the customer needs.

- Why would the customer want to use our product or service?
- Who cares about our offerings and what authority do they have?
- What is the level of financial authority required to approve our solutions?
- What is the impact of our offerings on our customer's customers, and how might we measure that?
- What are the best next actions that we can take to demonstrate the value of our offerings to our customer's key decision makers, and how do they align to the customer's business objectives?

Answers to these questions require the selling organization to change the focus of the lens they use to view the customer. It changes from product, price, and commodity to value, return, and a business relationship that will help the customer achieve key metrics. This will take many out of their comfort zone, but it is not an option if the objective is to change conversations, which will begin to change the value we can bring to our most important customers.

Customer-First Alignment

Managing effective customer relationships across the spectrum of a company's customer base as a democracy—one customer, one vote—is a sure recipe for disaster. We cannot be all things to all people. Customers do not want us to be all things to all people. They want a company to align resources to deliver solutions for *their* specific problems, not everyone's.

This process of identifying and balancing customer requirements with the selling resources of the firm is often called segmentation and coverage strategy. Companies do it every day, some better than others. Some are rather cavalier, "I have been at this for 10 years; these 10 customers dictate our strategy. They drive the market. What they require of us is what we will do for the rest of them." Some boil the ocean with analysis, and neglect to organize their strategies, campaigns, and selling resources in a sustainable manner—lots of analysis; no action.

At its base, segmentation starts with fact-based findings to the following questions.

- What are current revenue and profit streams from each customer?
- What logical groupings begin to cluster?
- What is the customer spending on competitive services and products?
- Are there similar themes of business issues that these clusters or segments are dealing with?
- If we were at our best, how would we most effectively align with each segment?
- What must we do to affordably market, sell, and deliver to each segment?
- In which segments do we want to invest and what resources would be required to develop new, profitable relationships and retain or expand current relationships?

There is an extensive body of thinking and experience about customer and market segmentation. For our purposes, we focus on the most important segment of clients or prospects that require and deserve our best people, thinking, and attention. Too often, selling organization enthusiasm for expanding into other segments dilutes focus on their make-or-break segment. After that segment and its team are performing well, we focus on the next segment. Success is contagious, but each segment has a different definition of success.

The next best practice is to begin to listen more intently to the voice of the customer. Again, there is a great deal of academic, professional, and anecdotal work in this area. Billions of dollars have been invested in quality and customer satisfaction research programs, especially since former Secretary of Commerce Malcolm Baldridge became a celebrity. We see clients make various levels of investments in these programs, with various levels of impact.

Our clients search for the voice of the customer in many ways.

- Focus groups
- Customer satisfaction surveys
- 1-800# and Web inquiry analysis
- Customer service metrics
- CRM systems analysis

Some of our clients do it the old-fashioned way with that most important segment we discussed earlier—they talk to them. When these exploratory conversations are at their best, they are different than they were several years ago.

- There are conversations at the executive as well as user levels
- Conversations are value-based versus cost-based
- Conversations are solution-based versus product-based
- Conversations are focused on creating competitive advantage for the customer and the customer's customer

All efforts to change conversations among selling organization members must be focused on the customer. When conversations are wrapped around customer outcomes, they change the way people see their role, their goals, and the best ways to achieve them. These internal conversations around the customer should occur on a business-to-business, solution or product offering, and person-to-person basis. Here are some example questions most likely to help refocus selling organization actions.

- What are the customer's most critical business needs (pains and gains)?
- What are the strengths of our offerings that can best serve those needs?
- What are the measurable benefits to the customer?
- What are compelling business reasons for the customer to consider our offering?
- Who cares the most about these benefits?

- What are our and the customer's best next actions that will generate a sense of urgency to proceed?

These types of questions focus salespeople on *discovering what the customer values*. This puts them in a better position to develop targeted value propositions and actions for particular customers. These conversations can lead to different actions, different thinking, and an entirely different selling organization.

Value Validation

What counts for both buyer and seller is not necessarily the value sales teams propose, but *what the customer acknowledges to be valuable*. No matter what efforts sales teams take to create value for customers, it will mean little to their success or to the customer unless it is confirmed. The value of an offering may be crystal clear to the seller, but without the customer's validation, the proposal may be ignored or treated as a commodity.

Ideally, sellers want the customer to be able to articulate the value of the offering to their company—in a simple phrase. "XYZ, with its unique capabilities, will help us reduce our overhead and allow us to provide more reliable service to our customers." When people on selling teams know the *value statement that they want their customer to speak*, they can set strategy to make it easy for the customer to put together a rationale to buy from their company.

> One manager at a company that sells software products and services realized that overreacting to price pressure was a cultural phenomenon the sales team had created with a particular large customer. She believed that this culture was established during ongoing conversations with the customers—had they only talked about price? She engaged the sales team in a *value-selling* program, and heard a litany of excuses about price.
>
> The manager hypothesized that the reason the team was grappling with price was that it was the focus of *their* conversations with the customer. Later, they admitted that their customer might value their product, in significant and quantifiable ways, and that their offering might deliver significant competitive differentiation—if they had a value-based conversation.
>
> The team reorganized their efforts to help this customer understand the value received from both the product and actions of the selling team. They also began to get formal agreement from the customer on

the offering's value and budget before entering into price negotiation. The sales team's conversation changed in these ways.

Changing Conversations

From	To
The buyers we talk to care only about price.	The buyers appreciate value when it is at the center of our discussion.
Our product is becoming a commodity.	Our solution is the highest quality and produces quantifiable results.
There is no budget for our products.	There is always money available for a solution that brings demonstrable value.

The sales team identified key business drivers for their customer's business, helped them to calculate potential bottom-line impacts, and developed a business case. As a result, a new budget was created for the solution, additional services and software were bundled into it, and the solution end users took an active part in acquiring the solution.

In 60 days, there was a much richer pipeline with larger transactions in every stage. In 120 days, the order backlog had doubled. In 180 days, the sales team realized higher profit and customer satisfaction as well as follow-on orders for additional products and services. They were also helping develop the customer's two-year strategy.

An interesting thing happens when sales teams are engaged in conversations that focus on value. They develop a passion for what they are doing, for finding what the customer values, for finding the best ways to serve the customer, and ultimately, a passion for winning. When that happens, the selling organization is on its way to differentiating its offerings in positive ways.

There is a bonus to driving desired selling organization changes through changed conversations. Leaders are able to transfer the best practices of their top one percent of performers to the rest of the organization *through customer-focused conversation.*

It is also important to use conversations to impart the passion and energy of sales leaders and salespeople to non-salespeople in the company. Non-sales colleagues will understand how they can play a key part in serving a particular customer.

Set Extraordinary Goals

The best way to start the journey toward extraordinary sales results is to develop extraordinary goals. This is not as far out as it may sound. If implemented correctly, it harnesses the energies of the selling organization as no other single factor can. Developing and striving toward an extraordinary goal is a powerful entrée to changing conversations with salespeople to work better and smarter for outcomes they would not otherwise imagine.

As CPS partner, Mike Morton, says, "Extraordinary results begin with extraordinary thinking and goals that lead to extraordinary actions. This does not mean just working harder or longer. It means everyone's efforts are focused on stupendous possibilities and performance. If a selling organization aspires to extraordinary sales results, they will behave differently to help stretch their performance."

An Action-Based Look at Achieving Extraordinary Results

Current Thinking →	Current Actions →	Current Results
▪ React to opportunity ▪ Fix everything ▪ Always closing ▪ Focus on internal issues ▪ Everyone has their own plan to meet ▪ Sales is not a process	▪ Reorganize every year ▪ Depend on top performers ▪ Have consultants analyze everything ▪ Set lower prices ▪ Set higher targets ▪ Acquire competitors ▪ Buy CRM software ▪ Partner with everyone ▪ Inspect after loss	▪ Long selling cycle ▪ Miss targets ▪ Lose best people ▪ Lose customer loyalty ▪ Low-profit sales
Extraordinary Thinking →	Extraordinary Actions →	Extraordinary Results
▪ It is all about the customer's success ▪ Exciting goals ▪ Everything is a project ▪ Selected milestones ▪ Focus on best next actions (BNAs) ▪ Management discipline ▪ Identify "big rocks" ▪ Focus on execution and accountability	▪ Clear priorities ▪ Documented, consistent sales process ▪ Consistent, targeted behavior of teams ▪ Progress through accountability ▪ Review of progress ▪ Cultivate wide range of customer relationships ▪ Calibrate success	▪ Create new blockbuster relationships ▪ Customers recognize value provided ▪ Focus on partners like customers ▪ Continue to enjoy successes in good times and in bad ▪ Prepared for next level

Achieving extraordinary results requires good planning and processes, management discipline, people management, and a relentless focus on execution and accountability.

A lot of careful work needs to be done initially to define the goal from all constituency views. Enrolling the team with collective enthusiasm is key. That extraordinary goal needs to be huge, but achievable, even if goal setters do not know exactly how just yet. Here are some suggested steps for shaping an extraordinary goal.

- Identify key business initiatives that the customer is investing in to improve performance. Identify these for each area of the customer's business that your products and services could impact.

- Identify your company's competencies that could most impact the customer's key initiatives.

- Identify people within the customer's organization who would reap the greatest benefit and who could influence the decision.

- Look for examples of other customers who have been successful. Discover what roadblocks they encountered and why they were successful.

- Brainstorm possible solutions and results, and refine them by enrolling your team and the customer into the goal.

There must be confidence on the part of those setting the extraordinary goal that they can develop a plan to pursue it. An extraordinary goal needs a targeted timeframe within which it can be accomplished so it appears manageable. With that in mind, continue defining and refining the goal.

- Define a goal significantly larger than what most people would believe possible; no lay-ups

- Make sure it is big enough so that the obvious path to it is "foggy"

- Stretch that goal and add certain characteristics that would make it extraordinary from both your company and the customer's perspective

- Expand and refine the goal for greater mutual results

- Communicate your vision until everyone feels the excitement

The extraordinary goal will continually stretch sales leaders and salespeople to explore ways of enlarging value for them and their customers, and to capture new opportunities they would not otherwise have entertained. An extraordinary goal represents more than a leap of faith and, as such, it goes beyond traditional parameters and everyday constraints. Pursued in the wrong way (through current thinking), an extraordinary goal is seldom achieved. Pursued with extraordinary thinking—starting with defining the best results for the customer—an extraordinary goal generates enthusiasm and better results every time.

Chapter Summary

Changing conversations to customer-first, aligning resources to the most important customers, articulating value in the context of the customer's business, and setting extraordinary goals will go a long way to changing behavior.

First and foremost in launching change management, the CSO must assess the culture and gauge the level of difficulty for change—usually a 10 on a scale of one-to-10. Using customer-first conversations will help keep the requirement for change externally focused rather than internally focused.

A company's most important segment of customers deserves its best people, thought leadership, and attention. The focus must be on discovering what the customer values, and validating it in their language.

Focusing on the customer is one thing. Focusing on extraordinary results for the customer is another. Extraordinary outcomes for customers mean extraordinary sales results for selling organizations. When an organization and its selling teams embrace an exciting extraordinary goal, the benefits of change far outweigh the risks.

5

Optimize Selling Operations

It's not the will to win that matters—everyone has that. It's the will to prepare to win that matters.

—Paul "Bear" Bryant

At CPS we work with many sales leaders who have been in their current positions for a short time, or are preparing for a new role and want to gain traction as quickly as possible. Our advice to them is the age-old axiom: *Knowledge is power*. We coach them to know their customers' business and then optimize that knowledge for peak performance.

This chapter speaks to knowing your customer, your people, your processes, your solutions, and your metrics; and optimizing your business models based on that knowledge. Many of our clients are quality-driven companies, having instilled Six Sigma, ISO, and other standards of quality. What all companies strive to achieve is consistent execution. What is sometimes missing is focus on doing the right things, not doing everything. Optimization is about doing what it takes to accomplish your goal based on the following sales steps of a critical path.

Step 1. Mapping from Sales Lead to Order: Know Your Customer

At the end of the day, no matter how complex or straightforward the solution, customers buy in a discrete buyer-seller engagement. Sellers may be involved in one selling engagement or a thousand, but each one is a single opportunity.

For this reason, they need to get to the transactional level to define their selling process. How do CPS clients go about *designing their sales process?*

The best way to design a sales process (from scratch or to optimize an existing process) is to begin with what the seller wants the customer to do, or agree to, or signal at each stage of the sales process. These are the seller's markers of progress and a green light to go to the next step; we call them customer outcomes.

A useful way to identify customer outcomes is to consider how target customers (the ones we selected in our segmentation exercise) would likely buy or prefer to buy from the selling organization.

- What stages does the customer go through in the process of making a purchase?
- What are the critical events that end one stage of the process and signal the readiness of the customer for the next one?

At the same time, sellers need to consider what they want to happen along the life of the transaction with a particular customer.

- What is a natural and logical progression of the selling organization and the buyer from initial contact to closing the sale?
- Do they want the customer to confirm that their value proposition is understood and acceptable?
- Are they seeking approval for technical specifications of their offering? Does it fit?
- Do they want the customer to agree to the scope, terms, and statement of proposed work?

These stages can be considered gates that the seller must pass through to the next point of consummating the sale. One such gate, for example, might be technical acceptance of an offering, signaling that the customer acknowledges that the company's product or offering will do what the customer wants it to do for them.

On the basis of this analysis, the team can identify customer outcomes that will guide the sales process through successive stages on the way to concluding a transaction. The outcomes themselves are those decision points, or go/no go points, that depend on the customer to acknowledge their agreement with that proposition, offering, or course of action.

Customer outcomes form the basis of the sales process that can effectively track to closure. They indicate that sellers can move to the next step in the process. They ultimately define the steps of the sale.

Example Sales Process Steps Outcomes

Step 1→	Step 2→	Step 3→	Step 4→	Step 5→
Customer agrees to first meeting	Customer concurs with value alignment, value statement, and decision date	Customer recognizes sales solution exceeds requirements and concurs with implementation plan	Customer reviews and understands proposal	Customer signs order

Key outcomes provide a two-dimensional view of the progress of the opportunity. These outcomes tell sellers whether they have achieved a landmark point of concurrence with the customer, and how well they have managed activities related to that outcome. Essentially, sellers have a customer-outcome view of what is transpiring. Next, sellers need to focus on the kinds of activities required to achieve those outcomes.

Define Best Practices that Most Effectively Support the Sales Process

Each step of the sale requires selling activities that will help to achieve the targeted customer outcome. What are the best kinds of activities at that step of the sale? Using customer outcomes as targets, sellers can identify critical actions that will move them steadily toward reaching those outcomes—the defining situation that tells them that they have moved a step ahead in closing that opportunity.

The best place to begin developing an effective sales process is to establish the general framework for the selling process. CPS clients focus on the five specific areas listed below to segment activities necessary to achieve the customer outcome from a specific sales stage.

1. Demonstrate company's capabilities
2. Communicate value of those capabilities
3. Build trust-based relationships
4. Establish clear, fair, commercial governing principles
5. Engage correct buying and selling team members at appropriate time

With the framework clearly established, the selling organization's best performers are tapped to discover what works best for them. Sales process developers should work backwards and dissect the elements of their organization's successes, asking questions such as the following ones.

- What did the selling organization's top one percent of salespeople do to reach their goals successfully?
- What are the characteristics of their most successful sales pursuits?
- How did they overcome hurdles?
- Are there repeatable patterns in their sales activities?

If sellers are in the proposal stage, for example, they want the customer to say, "We have received your proposal and understand your value proposition; your proposal meets [or exceeds] our expectations." What do sales teams have to do for the customer to say this? Process developers might ask the top one percent of salespeople these questions.

- What made you money at this stage?
- What were the essential elements of winning proposals?
- What did you do to exceed customer expectations?

Alternatively, if sales teams are at the point of expecting a signed purchase order, what are best practices for actions to take at this point—after they deliver and present the proposal, but before they get the order? These may include executive-to-executive contact, preparation work before negotiations, and customer testimonial about the company's speed to value realized. With this kind of information, developers can fill in best practices kinds of activities.

Criteria for Excellence

TRUST your pipeline. In 2003, CPS asked a new client, "Do you trust your pipeline?" Based on his response, CPS developed the following concept and framework. CPS clients continue to validate the appropriateness of the TRUST framework as the opportunity management discipline within their selling organizations. Fundamentally, TRUST is based on the following elements.

TRUST Framework

T	Technology Fit	Assure that the selling team demonstrates their technology solution is a fit for the customer
R	Relationship	Build the relationships necessary to accelerate the transaction through the pipeline
U	Utility (Value)	Communicate the utility or value of the solutions
S	Strategy	Introduce the strategy to win the opportunity
T	Team	Engage the selling and buying teams just-in-time, not just-in-case

There is one more sweep of design criteria required to make the sales process a high-performance tool for a group of high-performing sales individuals. Some people might call these the icing on the cake. We think of them more as the software for the process, or application programs, without which the hardware (process framework) will not do much.

Scope. Some sales activities appropriate for a certain step may need the participation of non-sales participants. They may involve commitments of resources (translation: funds), which are always scarce, and commitments of responsibility, which are usually tough to garner from people with day jobs. Developers must ensure that sales process activities properly reflect the required range of participation. As we suggested earlier, it is useful to have some of those individuals involved in the sales process development exercise.

Usability. No process, however solid or sophisticated, is worth much if the people for whom it is designed do not use it. The sales process needs to be simple, memorable, and useful for all participants.

In nearly any business today, virtual teams are commonplace. They have different educational and cultural backgrounds with different associated experiences. Despite the lack of proximity and because of the diversity, each virtual team member must absolutely understand his or her responsibilities in relation to the process.

Usefulness for participants and management coaching. Sales process developers should take care to ensure that the activities outlined are not over-complicated. People's time is valuable and they need to do what is useful for their work. Otherwise, they may ignore the process. Additionally, the process must scale to all types of transactions.

It is especially important to design the process so accountability for pipeline quality and responsibility for moving opportunities forward resides with first-line managers. They ultimately figure out how to get things done, well and on time, and are the sales leader's first indication of how well teams are performing. The managers use the sales process to understand the best practices, and devise best next actions to move forward. Process developers need to ask questions that will provide insightful responses.

- Are activities we identified helpful, or even useful, for first-line managers?

- Are the actions something they can use to manage and coach their salespeople and track progress?

- What kinds of activities could give them an advantage in doing what they need to do?

Optimization. If these criteria have been met, there is a final filter that developers must use to ensure the implementation quality of the sales process. Sales process developers need to check their creation to make sure that it is not an inflexible or unusable work of art that is more trouble than it is worth to apply.

The following table summarizes the attributes of a powerful, predictable, and optimized sales process.

Sales Process Criteria

Scalable	Accommodates all types of selling situations
Repeatable	Promotes consistent sales team actions without management intervention
Flexible	Accommodates various circumstances
Trackable	Contains easily monitored markers of progress
Coachable	Provides common language and best practices

The Finished Product

Here is an example of a completed sales process, with optional acronyms.

Sales Process Example

SELLING STAGE				
Prospect	Discover	Qualify	Propose	Close
TRUST ACTIVITIES				
First-level references	Identify business problem	Develop evaluation plan	Determine scope of solution	Negotiate pricing, terms, and conditions
Business development leads	Align core competencies with critical business problems	Construct specific demonstration	Allocate team resources	Communicate from company executive to customer executive
Business analysis	Confirm suitability of customer's supplier requirements	Validate technical architecture	Validate value alignment	Recruit executive sponsor to expedite paperwork and signature
Third-party lead generation	Determine if customer is open to different approach	Expand view of opportunity	Conduct customer "yellow pad" meeting	Reconfirm value recognition with customer
Gather general business background information	Present and demonstrate	Benchmark to competition	Complete contract with terms and conditions	Engage pre-sales and assign account manager
Capture information technology architecture	Assess integration requirements	Provide proof of concept, if required	Secure executive sign-off	Affirm customer delivery resources and/or partner resources assigned to implementation

SELLING STAGE				
Prospect	Discover	Qualify	Propose	Close
	Verify investment metric	Queue account management resource	Review proposal with customer	
	Determine customer buying process and technical and operational decision makers	Develop scope and urgency of implementation plan		
	Estimate technical investment required	Manage pre-sales call to technical decision maker		
	Develop and deliver value statement			
	Evaluate potential partners			
OUTCOMES				
Customer agrees to first meeting	Customer concurs with value alignment and value statement	Customer recognizes that solution exceeds requirements	Customer reviews and understands proposal	Customer signs order

What about the names of the steps of the sale? If everything else about the process checks out, developers can get creative. It is useful for the sales process to have an acronym, so people can remember it easily. As the usability criterion says, keep it simple and memorable. For example, a sales process that we have seen work effectively is called PEAC. For one organization, the letters signified the steps of Prepare, Explore, Activate, Close. For another, they meant Plan, Execute, Align, Confirm.

The sales process is the selling organization's touchstone for results. It promotes consistent actions, reduces friction and wasted effort, and concentrates attention on where attention matters—customer outcomes.

Benefits of a Good Sales Process

The discipline of a sales process allows everyone in the selling organization to have useful discussions about a particular customer, and get the best information on which to base their decisions. They can share information and insights, collaborate, and report progress. Their actions have more meaning.

By working through a defined sales process, selling organizations can validate the value offered and delivered to, and acknowledged by, the customer, at every stage in the process. For sales leaders, sales process steps allow them to do their job better, that is, managing selling activities. Through the sales process they can effect certain activities and actions with greater efficiency.

- Require salespeople to identify and take best next actions in sales activities
- Redirect salespeople to key sales actions, and recognize their performance
- Assess current resources assigned or needed for a particular sales initiative
- Bring new sales staff quickly into context so they can be effective earlier

Many key people in the company, both inside and outside the selling organization, rely on the sales process to focus their efforts. It gives people the same information about pipeline progress, allows them to contribute where it matters, and saves everyone time. Here is how some key players make good use of a sales process.

- **CEO**. Chief executives use information about pipeline forecasts to talk knowledgeably and credibly to investors and other stakeholders. Analysts expect CEOs to be able to provide data on predictable future earnings.
- **CFO**. The financial head of the organization depends on pipeline forecasts to develop financial forecasts and budgets for the company, and link financial implications of pipeline forecasts to capital and operational investments.

- **Functional business manager.** Managers of functional areas, like manufacturing, for example, rely on pipeline information to plan expenditures, deploy material and labor, and establish contract terms and timing.

- **Business unit manager.** Other business managers can take note of red flags in the sales process and realign resources accordingly, acting proactively rather than reactively.

- **Second-line sales manager.** These managers, even more than their business unit counterparts, have a direct need for sales process data to manage effectively and to direct resources where they are needed.

- **Sales manager.** With access to sales process and pipeline information, these first-line managers can more effectively transfer best practices where and when they are most needed.

- **Salesperson.** Individual salespeople can use sales process information as a reality check on their own activities, and as a spur to drive best next actions as they organize their time and efforts.

- **Non-salesperson.** Participants from other parts of the enterprise can better support the types of activities required at each stage of the sale with reliable and timely information about activities in the sales process.

- **Customer.** The customer values the consistent way that the selling organization sells to them. *These people do not waste my time.*

What this means is that both selling organization and business productivity can be improved. The discipline of a defined sales process has natural outgrowths that make the selling organization more productive in its activities and the whole enterprise more productive in its business.

If the selling organization can coordinate its efforts better, it is more efficient and effective. If the non-sales parts of the business can provide targeted assistance on the basis of a clear process, their contributions have more impact. Everyone's efforts become better aligned with those of others and overall productivity is improved. Coordinated use of a sales process has many beneficial aspects.

- Aligns planning processes and tools
- Effectively manages resource priorities and allocations
- Coordinates customer communications
- Identifies and reinforces marketing lead-generation requirements
- Streamlines decision-making

- Better qualifies opportunities at any point, and earlier
- Better uses selling organization resources for better results
- Better manages customer expectations to exceed them

Most sales leaders would find this list of benefits compelling. It is within their power to make big wins with focused use of a sales process. The mantra here is to develop the model, but keep it simple.

Step 2. Hire, Review, Promote, Turnover: Know Your People

Knowing what to ask of people, and knowing the gaps between what is asked and what they can get done, is a central tenet of successful sales management. The successful sales leaders we have observed have been diligent in defining the skill requirements to do the job they expect of individuals, assessing each individual contributor, providing personalized access for skills improvement, and establishing career paths and succession planning. Additionally, compensation and recognition plans must support the goals of the selling organization (consistent achievement of customer and management expectations) and each individual contributor (consistent achievement of personal financial and career goals).

At CPS, we work with hundreds of sales teams every year. We have seen the good, the bad, and the ugly of sales skills. Throughout our sales careers, we have noted a baseline set of skills that we have observed as critical to the success of a selling organization.

Business Acumen

- Understand customer's business and technology needs
- Analyze financial data
- Know business operations
- Negotiate effectively
- Plan and organize
- Improve processes continuously

Teamwork

- Demonstrate confidence and courage
- Lead virtual teams
- Demonstrate team and customer adaptability

- Influence without authority

Customer Focus

- Build trusted customer relationships
- Ensure customer satisfaction
- Demonstrate team and customer credibility and trust

Technical Knowledge

- Create effective solutions and customer-based value propositions
- Possess professional and technical knowledge of solutions

Communication

- Communicate effectively
- Present with impact

Once you identify skills needed in your sales organization, you must determine which of them reside within your organization.

Skills assessments take many forms. They may be completed by individual contributors, by their manager, or by their peers. Regardless of the source, each person must be periodically assessed and receive feedback on basic skills required to execute the company's sales strategy. The assessment process can be defined and accomplished in many ways.

At CPS, we believe that skill levels fall into one of four levels: Entry, Working, Senior, or Expert.

1. **Entry.** Minimal skills/knowledge, requires developing/coaching

2. **Working.** Understands basic skills/knowledge and applies with coaching and supervision

3. **Senior.** Applies basic skills/knowledge consistently with limited coaching and supervision

4. **Expert.** Role-model behavior, coaches others

These assessments provide you, the manager, a view of the current state of your selling team. Secondarily, your team should be asked how frequently they apply these skills in specific customer and internal team circumstances. We have tested the levels of using these skills with the following responses: never, seldom, regularly, frequently, and always.

The resulting analysis permits correlation between the skill level and the frequency of skill use. This triangulated assessment spurs personal development action. Skills that are seldom used combined with an entry skill level of understanding may not require immediate attention, whereas those skills that are used frequently or always and have low skill level ratings must be taught or relearned. Again, in this individualized culture, individual contributors must be respected for the knowledge and skills they possess, but also reminded of the skills that could be enhanced to become top performers.

Growing Sales Skills in a Growth Environment

A CPS client facing extraordinary growth pressures asked CPS to evaluate a worldwide group of account managers. The goal was to establish the appropriate curriculum that would generate the steep sales growth from existing customers that the company's leadership expected. Account managers participated in this evaluation through an online tool used for self-assessment. The results of the survey were communicated in the context of continuous improvement, and educational offerings were developed or acquired to address the most critical gaps. The company has continued to grow significantly through continuous expansion of its share of wallet from existing customers with growth of sales in excess of 35 percent.

Speaking of *perceived growth ceilings,* another client team was facing a 17 percent annual growth target from a customer who they believed had a 97-plus percent share of wallet. Crazy, you say? The account team sought out skills in business transformation and was able to clearly articulate the value it could bring to the customer, thereby expanding the wallet and subsequently closing the contracts necessary to achieve the growth target.

Continuous improvement in your selling organization is the only way your team will continue to exceed your expectations of them.

Assess Skills and Identify Training Gaps

Developing skill paths associated with the skills identified for your selling organization is the next step toward growing your team's performance capabilities. Aligning your skills matrix with available training courseware will help identify courseware white space that must be procured for your sales team.

Sales Skills Training Matrix

	Sales Skills Courseware Offerings				
	Basic	Business	Negotiate	Present	Account Manage
BUSINESS ACUMEN					
▪ Understand customer's business and technology needs	X	X	X	X	X
▪ Analyze financial data		X			X
▪ Know business operations		X			
▪ Negotiate effectively			X		
▪ Plan and organize	X				X
▪ Improve processes continuously		X			X
TEAMWORK					
▪ Demonstrate confidence and courage			X		X
▪ Lead virtual teams			X		X
▪ Demonstrate team and customer adaptability					X
▪ Influence without authority	X		X	X	
CUSTOMER FOCUS					
▪ Build trusted customer relationships	X		X	X	X
▪ Ensure customer satisfaction	X		X		
▪ Demonstrate team and customer credibility and trust	X		X	X	X

	Sales Skills Courseware Offerings				
	Basic	Business	Negotiate	Present	Account Manage
TECHNICAL KNOWLEDGE					
▪ Create effective solutions and customer-based value propositions		X		X	X
▪ Possess professional and technical knowledge of solutions		X		X	
COMMUNICATION					
▪ Communicate effectively	X		X	X	X
▪ Present with impact				X	

These training and coaching offerings can be provided in any number of ways. Depending on the size and sophistication of your sales and training organizations, e-learning, Web-based, facilitator-led, or one-on-one coaching can be used for training. One thing is critical to your success as a sales leader and will ensure a return on training your sales team: *Require first-line managers deliver some portion of the training.* Either through role-playing, coaching, or stand-up facilitation, change of behavior enabled by enhancement of skills will only become a reality when first-line management embraces and reinforces that behavior.

Once baseline skill assessments and curricula are in place, it is important to follow up with regular, periodic assessments based on performance data and qualitative judgment. These assessments provide you, the sales leader, with clear paths to improve the performance of your individual contributors, as well as your sales team in its entirety. Using skill assessments for succession planning and skills development will enable you to be prepared for inevitable changes that occur in sales organizations. Multinational companies rotate individuals through a number of assignments to better prepare them to be leaders of the future. Management expects its people to be prepared for change as well. Through regular assessments and continuous skills development, your organization can be a change agent in your company, not a victim of change.

Step 3. Commercial Processes: Know Your Processes

Selling is an art, not a science. How many times have you said this about yourself or your team?

Selling remains an enigma to many business leaders, and it has lagged becoming a major field of study in most universities across the globe. That is not to say that the chief financial officer is not interested in the process of order-to-cash, or that the chief operating officer is not interested in proof-of-concept to production, or that the chief marketing officer (CMO) is not interested in marketing campaign to closed customers. Everyone in the company is interested in the *results* generated by the sales organization, but not how they are achieved. Yet, high-performance selling organizations are focusing on the *how* in order to rapidly exploit competitive gaps and best practices.

Every selling organization has its processes, manual or automated, documented or intuitive, repeated or individually created. The most important element of your processes is the knowledge found in predictability, in discipline. Here are some of the most impactful processes within your selling organization.

- Segmentation and resource allocation
- Account management
- Customer relationship management
- Demonstration or proof-of-concept
- Proposal generation
- Pricing and negotiations
- Contract and order

To ensure your success as a sales leader, you must understand the systems and processes your teams are using to be successful and those that impede their productivity. Your job is to provide actionable processes and tools that align the critical thinking of your sales team with the objectives set by management.

Segmentation

As we discussed earlier, customer segmentation lies at the heart of successful selling organizations. It drives your coverage model, including sales team deployment, territory assignments, inside or outside sales coverage, or channels or direct coverage. While many practices are deployed for segmentation, we at CPS see a small number of common themes. What are the determinants?

- Addressable share of customer's wallet (potential revenue or reward)
- Company's ability to execute (product, services, and resources)

Of course, many other criteria influence the decision, including profitability of the customer to your company relationships, reference ability, and geographic accessibility. The critical point is to establish criteria for your organizational unit and apply them consistently.

In the segmentation model, the upper right hand quadrant segments those customers where competencies (ability to execute) align with the customer's business for extraordinary rewards.

Segmentation Matrix

<u>II.</u> • Inside sales coverage • Partner to improve execution ability	<u>I.</u> • Field sales coverage • Alliance partners
<u>IV.</u> • Channel partners • Disinvest	<u>III.</u> • Low-cost coverage model

High↑ ... Reward ... Low↑

Low→   Ability to Execute   →High

Here are the steps to activate segmentation.

- Determine metrics for each axis; we recommend that no more than five elements be considered under reward factors and ability to execute factors
- Apply criteria rigorously across geography and review with team
- Develop sales coverage and approaches for each quadrant
- Execute to the sales approaches and review segmentation quarterly

This approach can be used at the territory, district, region, and geographic or industry level, and will provide the basis for effective deployment and management of your team.

Account Management

The account management process within selling organizations enables a consistent, predictable set of actions and deliverable value to your customers. The scope of account management includes all interactions between your company and your customers. The goal of any account management process is to exceed commercial goals your company has for a customer, while delivering value in excess of the customer's expectations at every encounter. During the process, prepare for a long-term relationship with your customers, establish commercial and relationship goals, explore for high-value solutions, and establish action plans to deliver value to your customers and sales to your organization.

To deliver this value and exceed your customers' expectations, include the following components in your action plans.

- Environmental and historical account information
- Value delivered and value potential
- Opportunities to provide additional solutions
- Relationship assessment and plans
- Goals and action plans

All selling organizations are unique and the account management process and implementation requires some degree of customization.

You will be successful when account management teams, collectively and individually, understand the goals, agree on the value to be delivered, are accountable for major milestones, and know what the most important best next action is to accomplish a given milestone or build a critical relationship. We will discuss account management execution in more detail later.

Other Critical Processes

Several CPS clients have taken the step of establishing best practices groups within their sales departments. These groups capture, codify, and scale repeatable best practices across the company. CPS highly recommends that a program of sharing and deploying best practices be institutionalized within your organization. The idea is intuitively obvious; its activation requires intentionality and commitment. One of our clients uses every sales meeting as a forum for best practice discussions, asking a high performer to share a best practice with the team.

> To create a coaching environment within a selling organization, and leverage the best ideas in use at the company, a CPS client deployed a

best practices unit within its selling organization. The group is staffed with successful sales individuals whose career track is headed toward higher management. An agent of change throughout the organization, the best-practices group provides coaching to drive results and engages with field sales teams to explore applying these proven best practices.

Step 4. Product/Services Offerings Mapping: Know Your Solutions

We all recognize that very successful companies have differentiated products or services that set them apart in the marketplace. But as the solutions mature and the product/services offerings widen, the ability to articulate the value of the breadth of solutions becomes significantly more complex. As salespeople, we are asked to sell the breadth of our product line yet, in fact, we have selective experience in selling a particular product or service.

In order to enable a high-performance sales team, we must be able to clearly communicate the value of our offerings so it is understood by our customers. We see selling organizations across the globe simplifying an ever-increasing complex set of solutions. The approaches taken generally fall along two separate but similar tracks.

Solution framework. Activating a solution framework process for your selling organization is a critical component of your go-to-market processes. A solution framework will benefit your sales team and your customers. Given sales goals to establish a beachhead within new customers or gain additional share of wallet from your existing customers, your team must systematically view customers through the broader lens of your entire solution set. The solution framework will provide that lens. Here is an example.

> A division of a leading supply chain services company concluded that it was an under-recognized participant in a $1-trillion-plus industry. In order to communicate the breadth of its capabilities to customers, the sales leadership developed a client services framework. The framework provided context for account teams to begin to understand the scope of the industry in which this division was operating. The critical issue became, "Can customer-facing account teams recognize growth opportunities for our division, and at the same time deliver world-class service to our customers?" The client services framework became the single communication point that each team member could reference to understand the depth of the solution being provided. Likewise, it highlighted

the potential for growth beyond the currently delivered solutions—the customer white space.

All selling teams recognize that selling the entire portfolio of solutions is critical to their companies' success, but each member of the team has varying confidence in a given capability or solution. The solution framework encourages discussions of what is possible, both internally and with customers. Once the team and your customers understand what is possible, then the selling begins.

Solution value chain. Implementing solution value chains will increase the courage and confidence of your sales team, enhancing their ability to deliver messages that are heard, messages that stick to your customers. We have helped develop value chains for clients that target specific positions within their customers. The solution value message to the CFO is generally significantly different from the message for the COO, which may be different from a business unit executive. The critical point is to provide your sales team with crisp, differentiated messages that will be heard by customers.

As an example, CPS' value chain messages follow. The process includes core values, the benefit to customers, core competencies, and key messages.

Critical Path Strategies' Value Chain

CPS CORE COMPETENCIES	
Value Creation	We focus on creating recognizable value for clients, our firm, and our stakeholders by aligning our capabilities with our clients' critical business drivers.
Client Focus	In all that we do, our clients are our number one priority.
Responsiveness	Our operating principle is to provide just-in-time customized response to client needs. Internally, we communicate as if our lives depended on it.
Respect	We respect clients' culture and intelligence; internally, we treat each member of our firm with respect.
Account Management	We deliver client value through implementation of best practices for sales organizations.
Integrity	We live what we recommend. We do what we say. We strive to exceed clients' expectations of CPS.
Expertise	We are committed to attracting, retaining, and further developing extraordinary people.
Teamwork	We are dedicated to the attainment of the team's extraordinary goals.
Positive Work Environment	We strive to minimize the number of bad days and moments through our attitude and actions.
Who We Are	Since 1992, CPS has been helping clients gain momentum and achieve market traction for their most valued customers.
What We Do	CPS specializes in helping clients implement customer-focused strategic initiatives, including account management execution. We also offer comprehensive consulting services designed to align management teams around critical strategy and relationship initiatives. Our goal is to create recognizable value for clients through a coordinated, strategic approach to their most important needs.

VALUE-ADDED BENEFITS		
• Achieve top-line sales growth, account penetration, and customer satisfaction that consistently exceed expectations by implementing CPS tools and methodologies • Build high-value relationships, expand sales opportunities, increase sales team confidence, and grow top-line revenue within most important accounts through pervasive implementation of best practices for sales organizations • Achieve momentum, alignment, and traction through a coordinated, strategic approach to most important initiatives		

Beneficiaries	• Business Executives • Management Teams • Relationship Managers • Account Managers	• Team Leaders • Sales Representatives • Product Specialists • Marketing

CORE COMPETENCIES	
Best-Practices Based Processes (create Thought Leadership)	CPS partners and principals have broad experience in developing, refining, and implementing critical processes. Our experience in successfully implementing processes and over-arching management discipline has been refined through comprehensive research of best practices in leading organizations.
Strategy Development and Activation (facilitate Thought Leadership)	Extensive facilitation experience enables CPS partners and principals to facilitate highly effective strategy sessions. Our facilitation expertise enables clients to align management teams within a company, single business unit, or cross-business with critical initiatives that drive more effective use of resources, increased accountability, and extraordinary results.
Selling Organization Development (transfer and imbed Thought Leadership)	Years of selling and sales management experience enable CPS to provide effective methodologies to expand sales opportunities and provide world-class account management. Implementation of our critical thinking tools and approaches increases team confidence and helps build high-value executive relationships with most important customers.

Relationship Management	At the heart of CPS' processes and critical thinking tools is unwavering focus on creating mutual value in business relationships. Our ability to examine critical business relationships between an organization and its most important stakeholders—internal or external—enables the identification, alignment, and activation of projects that recognize mutual value.
KEY MESSAGES	
Value Proposition	We enable our clients to generate 100 to 500 times CPS fees in revenue growth by developing a strong global selling organization and activating customer-focused initiatives through scalable, efficient, and repeatable processes.
Consulting	We deliver customized consulting services designed to align management teams around critical selling organization initiatives. Our approach is a hard-hitting, results-focused engagement designed to yield the greatest return with the least total cost. We bridge the gap between strategy and results.
CSO Agenda	A model and framework to help select and activate the most important initiatives that enable a client to create recognizable value for their customers and themselves.
Account Management	Processes and tools to enable members of the selling team to increase their effectiveness by creating repeatable strategies and actionable plans around key accounts.

The ease with which your teams and your customers can understand your solutions and their attendant value can significantly enhance the scope of your influence with your customers. Successful sales teams look for their customers' unmet needs and meet them.

Step 5. Business Reporting: Know Your Results

What are the critical metrics for you as a sales leader in your organization? We understand there are leading indicators, in-process indicators, and lagging indicators in everything we do. The question is, what are the right metrics for your company? We would suggest it is a combination of all three types of metrics. We will begin with the end in mind.

Lagging indicators. One of our clients calls this *steering by our wake*. These are fairly straightforward metrics, most derived from the income statement and usually include a recap on a monthly or quarterly basis of the following measurements.

- Revenue results
- Profitability results
- Sales expense results
- Plan versus actual
- Customer retention
- Employee turnover

In-process indicators. These require some sales process definition and their veracity depends on the rigor of the process.

- *Pipeline.* Volume by stage and velocity of transactions
- *Quota performance.* By salesperson, sales manager, and business unit
- *Demonstrations.* Type and number of demonstrations completed
- *Proposals.* Size, number, and solution mix

Leading indicators. These are a bit more difficult and subjective but nonetheless critical.

- *Lead generation.* Quantity of qualified leads delivered to sales force
- *Marketing events.* Customer attendance at planned events
- *Customer satisfaction.* Customer acknowledgement of your company's value
- *Market share.* Competitors vis-à-vis your company
- *Web site.* Number of hits

Many of our clients translate these metrics into dashboards for rapid, visual, high-impact communications.

Chapter Summary

These steps (and best practices) more clearly define the required selling process around customer behaviors and desired outcomes to optimize business operations and keep the focus on delivering value to the customer.

- **Mapping from sales lead to order.** Know your customers and how they buy.
- **Hire, review, promote, turnover.** Know your people. Do they possess the skill set critical to success with customers?

- **Commercial processes**. Know your processes. CSOs must understand what they are asking their sales teams to do and how they are asking them to operate.
- **Product/services offerings mapping**. Know your solutions.
- **Business reporting**. Know your results. Measure meaningful metrics.

6

Transform Sales Teams

I believe the real difference between success and failure in a corporation can be very often traced to the question of how well the organization brings out the great energies and talents of its people.

—*Thomas J. Watson, Jr.*

You will recall the segmentation model in the previous chapter. The upper right hand quadrant segmented those customers where competencies (ability to execute) aligned with the customer's business for extraordinary rewards. This segment demands *platinum* coverage by effective sales teams. Democratic coverage, that is one customer equals one resource, is not sufficient. These customers require well-oiled selling teams.

To extend customer-first conversations into organizational reality, our clients frequently reorganize themselves into customer-focused teams. One highly silo-centric telecommunications organization believed that its perceived value would be enhanced if silo-specific salespeople were redeployed onto customer-dedicated teams. This was part of their *oneness* effort to deliver client-focused solutions, which were constructed with capabilities from multiple silos. Results? In one short year these teams put the company back on its growth path.

Activating the selling organization means having teams, structures, and processes in place so that the teams themselves are ready to take on responsibilities. The end result of the selling organization's activities depends on how well the whole sales organization behaves relative to its objectives. Have we taken the right actions for the desired outcomes? Are we consistently exercising best practices to bring optimum rewards for the customer and the selling organization?

When we refer to best practices, we mean applying *well-tested actions that are most appropriate to the situation*—so well timed and so well executed that they effectively advance an agenda. Best practices in sales can drive activity in the sales pipeline, build fruitful relationships, or more effectively solve customer problems. In this chapter, we will review how highly effective sales teams manage themselves. If the CSO can inject these team management mechanics into the sales culture, the teams will perform. If not, we will see teams spending a lot of time talking to each other rather than to the customer.

Establishing Effective Teams

In today's world, most important selling pursuits or sales projects are accomplished not by individuals, but by many people, some under a sales leader's control, but most outside that control. Despite the hope of many managers, the vast majority of *successful teams do not self-form*. Some gifted individuals do have natural instinct and energy to work collaboratively, but that is not the norm. Getting teams working well together is one of the most difficult and important jobs of sales management.

Why are cross-functional teams so important in a selling organization? The simple answer is that there is no other way to do what needs to be done. In the face of white-hot competition, complexity, and economic swings that are a part of commercial life, every selling organization needs the best resources it can muster, both inside and outside the selling group, in order to be effective. Few people, these days, are available full-time for anything.

We suggest you focus on three areas when forming teams.

1. **Make sure the reason is important according to the customer's definition.** Everyone knows that teams in selling organizations are formed for different purposes, at different times, and at different levels. Customer-facing teams can form around a specific sales opportunity/solution, market, or account relationship.

2. **Pick the right people.** Be selective about the composition and number of teams that are established. Sales teams should be formed to address the short list of the most important priorities of the selling organization. Each team, for each purpose, needs to have the right constituents—people with the required talents and people from appropriate functional groups. Each team needs an *owner*—the team leader or project manager.

3. **Communicate the importance of the team.** To establish sales teams around priority selling objectives, the CSO must mandate this team environment.

In our experience, effective sales leadership recognizes and leverages the unique qualities that each sales team member brings to the job. For example, if you find that one member of your sales team is particularly good at negotiating, enroll that member to take on that responsibility for the team. As subject-matter expert, that member will also coach the team on negotiating best practices.

How Top Teams Work

Teams that accomplish extraordinary sales results treat every sales campaign like a project. They develop specific milestones to accomplish a certain goal, identify short-term actions that lead them to achieve those milestones, and assign and enforce accountability for actions to which they have agreed.

No matter how much information top-shelf project teams begin with, it is highly likely that they will make hundreds of course corrections over the life of the sales campaign. However, they constantly move forward, persistently and effectively. What pushes them forward, in spite of obstacles, corrections, setbacks, and even failures?

World-class teams typically have an exciting, compelling vision and have determination to focus on short-term actions leading to the goal. We have all been on successful teams, and unfortunately, we probably have also been on dysfunctional teams. We assert that the following team mechanics must be in place, in order for the team to operate successfully.

- Everyone on the team clearly understands the overall goal, which is exciting and challenging from the customer's and sales team's viewpoint.
- Everyone on the team knows how the team will get there, and what part they will play.
- Everyone on the team knows his or her accountabilities to action.
- The project leader refines the strategy and work plan on the basis of new information and the knowledge gained from progress to date.
- The project leader communicates effectively, securing commitment of actions and holding people accountable for those actions.

Milestones. A critical team best practice is to identify a specific goal that will have significant benefit to the customer and is framed in a way the team believes is attainable. If a goal is too small, it does not generate excitement; if it is too large, people will not try.

While extraordinary goals are great for stretching thinking and providing something for which to strive, most people on a team cannot stay energized and focused for long periods of time on something that is too big or too distant. Most people need line-of-sight targets that are reachable and achievable so that they can pace themselves to the larger goal. These pacing targets, or milestones, form the framework of an action plan for moving toward the larger goal.

There is seldom just one solution to a complex situation. Getting team consensus on a few milestones required to accomplish the goal increases team members' confidence of success. Experienced sales professionals know that if the team understands how their individual actions relate to the milestones (and how those relate to the extraordinary goal), they will be much more likely to execute those actions. This is a proven method for pacing targets.

- Identify objectives and obstacles to overcome in order to reach a particular goal (Example: Clearly demonstrate how our capabilities will reduce cost and provide a technical fit)

- Identify key milestones (no more than eight to 10) and due dates required to at least barely achieve the objectives and overcome the obstacles necessary to accomplish the goal

- Spread milestones fairly evenly across the sales cycle (not clustered very early or very late)

- Assign responsibility for completion of each milestone to a team member

In most cases, salespeople typically do not know all the relevant information needed to develop a detailed project plan. They do know, however, that the situation will change (sometimes substantially) during the sales cycle. Rather than following a large static work plan, sales organizations should be guided by a *living plan*, one that is flexible enough to respond to new situations and information. In the continuum of milestones on the way to a larger goal, we recommend that sales leaders take certain actions.

- Adjust milestones and especially day-to-day actions related to each milestone as the situation changes.

- Delete milestones that are no longer relevant or that have been achieved, and focus on those that are best suited to attaining the project goal in light of current status.

- Regularly communicate with team members to review progress and invite suggestions.

In our experience, these sales campaign milestones typically fall into the first four categories of the TRUST model introduced in Chapter 5. The fifth category, teamwork, is the vehicle to accomplish the milestones.

1. **Technology Fit.** We must demonstrate that our offering is a technical fit for the client and that we can de-risk nightmares.

2. **Relationship.** What level of trust must we establish with which people in order to be successful?

3. **Utility (Value).** We must demonstrate that the fit or solution we bring yields demonstrable utility in the client's definition of value.

4. **Strategy.** We understand how the customer's buying process works and honor that process with an effective strategy.

5. **Teamwork.** We identify and enroll the selling team and get them aligned with the customer's buying team.

Focus on short-term actions. Sales leaders want the team to be committed to accomplishing an extraordinary goal, but focused tactically on the milestones. To encourage this, teams identify at least one short-term action for every milestone in the work plan—even for those milestones that are many months out. We call them *best next actions.* These answer the question, "What small action can we take to move the ball forward?" This is about continuous traction.

Short-term actions are the most effective use of team time. Like a weather forecast, for which a shorter duration increases the accuracy of the prediction, a shorter window of activity is likely to yield the best results. This is because situations will very likely change, and because we learn more about any situation as we act on it.

Early *right actions* make it easier to accomplish future critical milestones and prepare the team for unforeseen issues that arise later.

Accountability. These days more than ever, if it is not on the calendar it probably will not happen. It is disappointing to see how many people make promises with no discipline in setting a due date with accountability. The good news is busy people and, in fact, especially busy people, will honor their accountabilities to a well-managed team with an important goal. The team expects the leader to follow up on activities that were promised. If there is no follow-up, the leader's credibility suffers and the project will lose energy. Consider the following tips.

- Team members commit to dates and ensure that there is one person responsible for accomplishing each milestone and each best next action.

- Regular communication about the work plan and progress is critical. This will keep traction and establish best next actions based on that traction.

- Always set the date and time for the next follow-up discussion of the work plan. Keep these short (15 to 30 minutes is a best practice) and to the point. Short, frequent discussions seem to work best.

Priorities. The business environment is changing fast, dramatically, and in so many ways that individuals and teams find it difficult to work according to plans that were prepared even a short time earlier. Surprises constantly upset everyone's assumptions and plans for becoming successful.

There is no longer time for a sense of pause and reflection for a customer-facing team when the environment changes. That means they must be prepared to respond quickly, at every level. Teams that are prepared to respond survive profitably during the unplanned downturns, and readily grasp the opportunity of unplanned upturns.

Making time for what matters. How do high-performance people and teams manage time? Time management experts use a simple model comprising four areas where people spend their time. The following chart captures how we spend our time. We all are responsive to important and urgent quadrant I issues. Frequently, our time is robbed by less important (to us) quadrant III and IV activities.

Because of their lack of urgency, quadrant II activities (important but not urgent) are frequently shelved. However, successful teams and individuals regularly commit some of their time and share of mind to best next actions related to these activities. Teams can improve over time *only* if they commit some time "off the top" for these activities.

Time Management Matrix

	Urgent	Not Urgent
Important	Quadrant I • Customer satisfaction • Critical situation • Competitive situation • Financial deadline • **Best Next Actions**	Quadrant II • Relationship-building • Team communication • Personal development • Planning • Strategy development
Not Important	Quadrant III • Expense reports • Requests without context • Someone else's problem • Some e-mail • Forecasting	Quadrant IV • Rumors • Most e-mail • Most news

Adapted from Steven Covey, *The 7 Habits of Highly Effective People*

The project management discipline we spoke of earlier helps solve this dilemma. Otherwise, literally all of our time is absorbed in responding to daily, less important activities or others' priorities. These kinds of activities are characteristic of quadrants I, III, and IV. *Only quadrant II activities lead to steady improvement and activities that enable extraordinary results.*

What happens if teams continue business as usual, absorbed in quadrant I, III, and IV activities, and do not get to quadrant II initiatives except when everything else is complete? They keep reorganizing, cutting costs, and missing opportunities—until they no longer exist.

On the other hand, it turns out that many small, intentional, and calendared best next actions to address important quadrant II activities keep many of the quadrant I, II, and III issues from ever occurring! And when they do, they take much less time to address. In other words, the investment of time and share of mind on best next actions focused on quadrant II costs much less and supports much larger results.

Chapter Summary

Successful selling organizations have their best possible sales teams focused on their most important customers. Increasingly, these teams comprise members from functions outside a sales leader's control.

Team selling is critical. The more complex the solution, the more essential team selling is for success. Forming effective teams aligns *right-skilled* salespeople with customer needs.

High-performance teams are focused on the customer—not just responsive, but proactive. The team defines an extraordinary goal that demands creativity and performance. They create a plan to support the goal and a road map for achieving it. They know the dynamics for achieving it. They know the dynamics of the client and of the plan. Each team member is accountable—for their own assigned tasks and to one another. They communicate regularly with one another on plan status and are prepared for change if warranted.

Managing priorities and time is difficult. Time, enthusiasm, and energy are precious commodities. Carving out time and mind share on important/not urgent selling activities is a team best practice.

7

Connect Sales with Marketing and Customer Service

Coming together is a beginning, staying together is progress, and working together is success.

—Henry Ford

What Is the Message?

There are two aspects to managing the seller's message to the buyer. One is the message that the selling team manages in customer-facing interactions. The other is the marketing message that the selling company's marketing specialists craft to enhance the company's opportunities and reputation. The two messaging efforts should be "joined at the hip."

Unfortunately, this is not the case at a large number of companies that otherwise have good business practices. In our experience, the relationship between the marketing executive and the top sales executive is often cordial, but sometimes not collaborative. In fact, much too often we have observed that the business interaction between the CMO and the CSO is disjointed.

Marketing. Frequently marketing executives are frustrated by the selling teams' seeming disregard for communication standards and guidelines, which marketing believes protect and enhance the company's brand. Marketing people tend to think they have superior insights into the market and believe that sales should follow their lead. They talk a lot about *positioning* in the marketplace.

Sales. In a similar vein, selling executives often dismiss the marketing function as being generators of irrelevant fluff. Salespeople often consider much of what marketing does as soft and lacking accountability. Sales owns the relationships and they are going to keep it that way. Instead of positioning, they talk more about *penetrating or expanding* into specific customers.

The unfortunate result is that these two organizations frequently ignore the relationship breakdown and simply go their separate ways, often to the detriment of customers who have no filter to figure out what is relevant and important. These are functional groups that, superficially at least, pursue the same goal—customer trust, mind share, and share of wallet.

Most salespeople subscribe to the view that a company's value resides in its sales pipeline. Marketing professionals argue that a company's value is in its brand. We believe that they are both right, and when they are engaged it is a beautiful thing!

Cross-Border Agreements: Managed Messages

Sales and marketing need each other, and they each have obligations toward the other. More than that, they can each bring particular benefits to the other, if they work cooperatively.

Sales. For its part, the selling organization needs to do some due diligence to establish and codify a clear sales process (discussed in Chapter 5), which is the root of its value creation process. In fact, once developed and deployed, the sales process forms the basis of what can be a rewarding, collaborative working relationship between sales and marketing functions.

The selling team also needs to identify the specific kinds of help they require from marketing, such as particular sales tools for each step of the sales process. However, marketing should not be expected to reinvent these for each specific opportunity. The sales team's job is to apply these tools at the customer level to get the job done—one customer at a time. Sales teams create customer-specific, not industry-specific, solutions.

That is a job for marketing—to determine how the company's solutions address the needs of a particular industry or business function. In an ideal world, as the sales group uses their time to prospect and support customers, marketing can supply sales-ready material to the selling team to support each step of the sale.

Marketing. Marketing is the keeper of brand messages. Unfortunately, sometimes marketing people forget that their customers are not just markets, but that sales is also their customer. Accordingly, a legitimate part of marketing's job is to identify how to provide selling tools and material to help sales teams be effective.

Moreover, the programs and material that marketing provides need to be carefully targeted at particular audiences. They also need to be extremely practical and useful. Instead of having glossy brochures, for example, most salespeople would benefit more from material focused on real business problems and success stories. That is where marketing can leverage sales resources.

We believe that the development of a collaborative relationship between sales and marketing should begin with leaders in both functional groups having regular discussions as colleagues about their mutual goals, what each can do and needs to do for the other. Then more people from each group can become involved in defining business-specific and sales-specific material for selling teams. The respective commitments could be something along these lines.

- **Sales.** We will manage the selling teams so they adopt marketing's messages and adhere to communication standards. Here is the selling collateral sales teams need to support our sales process.

- **Marketing.** Here is what sales can count on from us and the feedback we need to improve.

If It Is a Message, Call Marketing

The selling team is responsible for its resources to ensure that every one of its members clearly understands the short-term sales agenda. Sales leaders must make it clear what is involved in this effort and what is expected of everyone. We have observed in particularly complex pursuits that the sales messaging plan needs some focus. A logical partner to enroll in this team effort is the marketing communications function.

A marketing communications professional can help develop a specific communication strategy and execution plan—whether for the customer sales team level or at the CSO level when a major agenda change needs to be announced and implemented. In fact, the marketing team can—and should—be the sales executive's most valuable tool in ensuring that the vision is clearly and consistently communicated and reinforced to customer-facing teams, the customer support team, and other company employees.

> Recently, CPS was engaged by the CSO of a global services company to help him determine why his newly launched strategic account management initiative was foundering.

In the year since he joined the company, Jim had analyzed the sales process and spent a great deal of time—and money—in assessing how best to drive results with key strategic clients. He developed a new customer engagement model and validated it through focus groups with customers and internal employees. The initiative, however, was failing in practice.

The field sales teams—and their managers—were avoiding the carefully developed and expensive training sessions to activate the model. The reports he wanted on a regular basis from the managers were not being submitted in a timely fashion; the quality of the forecasting was not improving. Jim was deeply puzzled and pretty aggravated. After discussing this with Jim, we had a good idea of what happened.

Jim had such a clear view of the benefit of the approach to his clients that he overlooked the fact that he had not brought the rest of the selling organization up to his level of understanding. Essentially, Jim was standing at the top of a mountain and could see clearly in all directions, but the selling organization—the selling team members, managers, sales representatives, customer support representatives, technical support personnel, and other customer-touching team members—could not.

To the customer-facing selling teams, the expensive training was just another program-of-the-day, to be tolerated but not embraced. They did not understand the context or potential impact of the model. Although this was a tough pill for Jim to swallow, we recommended that he relaunch the customer engagement model and treat it as the most important product launch he would do that year.

He also needed to step back and assess the roles in the product launch. Although he was the expert in establishing the selling team vision, he nevertheless needed an ally who was an expert in communication tactics. In this case, his best ally was the director of marketing communications, who helped map an effective strategy for successfully reintroducing this important sales initiative. This time it stuck.

Launching a new CSO agenda is critical and is analogous to launching a new product. Using the world of technology, for example, products are introduced to the marketplace that create value for the user. This company process integrates the voice of the market and the voice of the technology provider in analyzing, planning, and investing the firm's customer resources, policies, and activities. The purpose of this process is grounded in satisfying the needs of chosen customer groups at a profit.

In a similar vein, the CSO is launching a new product, his agenda, to a selected group of employees. Just as the launch of a new technology product is grounded in the wants and needs of chosen customer groups, so should the launch of the CSO agenda be grounded in connecting the needs of employees to the needs of the customers. What are the different employee constituent groups? Are there channel groups or suppliers who will be affected? What is their role in supporting the agenda? What message needs to be conveyed? How should the message be delivered to each group? What type of reinforcement is necessary? What deliverables should be provided?

The launch of the sales agenda should be planned and carefully managed and the best partner for this is the marketing function.

Process Recommendations for Internal Communications and Initiative Launch

There is nothing new or revolutionary here, just a set of reminders on how to introduce a culture-changing process. We helped Jim, the CSO whom we mentioned earlier, lay out an effective internal launch plan.

- Engage a marketing communications professional to help develop a communications strategy and execution plan. This must be treated as a communications project.

- Carefully assess the characteristics of the team to be impacted and determine their preferred way of receiving communication. Who are the team members? What are their roles and client responsibilities? What is the best way to interact with them? Web? E-mail? Webinars?

- Identify role models to become internal champions for the initiative.

- Immerse the management team first in the project; make sure they understand their roles as coaches and process leaders.

- Condition the field with appropriate customer messages before trying to send the team to any training sessions. Answer these questions—What? Why? How? Who? When?

- Be visible in leadership; model the behavior.

- Inspect what you expect, reward the role models, retool the naysayers.

- Communicate as if your life depended on it—because it does.

The External Launch

We said earlier that the value of a company is directly related to the quality of its pipeline. While that certainly rings true, marketing professionals would argue that a company's value is in its brand. Pundits have debated for years how best to ascribe financial value to a brand name. It is hard to argue, however, what happens when a brand loses its luster. All one needs to do is look at how quickly the fortunes of Enron and Arthur Andersen evaporated overnight when their companies became inextricably and undeniably linked with malfeasance and scandal. With that said, the simple fact is that the value of your brand is a function of the associated perceptions of your external stakeholders—analysts, stockholders, customers, employees, current/prospective customers, and suppliers.

What companies often overlook is that one of the primary vehicles for carrying the brand messages is the customer-facing team. If you subscribe to the belief that the value of the brand has a tangible impact on the fortunes of the company, it should be critically important to make sure that the right messages about your company are delivered to customers on a consistent basis.

Sales can advance marketing's efforts to promote and protect the company's brand. When sales teams promote the company's brand through their daily work, there are big benefits for the company and the selling organization. The brand comes to life.

For its part, marketing can provide sales with ready-made and approved material specifically targeted to industries, organizations, and roles within organizations. It is a way for marketing to have quality control over on-target content, but also to elevate its credibility by providing relevant and realistic material to those who need it to sell the company's offerings.

Customer Service and Sales Support

The link between sales and marketing is critical. Just as critical is the link between sales and customer service. As customers, immediately after the sale, our expectations will never be higher and the selling company's ability to execute will never be lower. The value proposition so eloquently crafted and delivered frequently is not realized. Perhaps it was not fulfilled because of one of the following issues.

- The sales team did not communicate it to the customer service/delivery team.
- The customer service/delivery team did not accept its responsibility.

- The customer service/delivery team had conflicting performance metrics.

- The customer service/delivery team processes were not designed to support *customers for life*.

We all know that customer service and sales support is critical to the health of our selling organization and to the profitability of our business. Poor customer service results in loss of customers and difficulty in obtaining new customers, profitably. Good customer service is highly valued by customers in today's environment and is critical to every supplier who intends to survive and thrive. We cannot get along today with sloppy or even mediocre service.

> As vice president of sales for a large environmental management company, CPS partner, Ken Evans, focused understandably on sales priorities like sales process, people-to-people effectiveness, and business-to-business relationships. New customer selling rates began to gain momentum and felt good. Then he began noticing some disturbing developments. The company was losing more customers than it was gaining. The lost customers were profitable ones and the new ones less so. Competitors were chewing into their profitable customer base and revenues.
>
> The firm launched some customer satisfaction research. It was ugly. The worst news by far was that the company was actually unresponsive to its dwindling set of customers. Unresponsive! The firm responded with an in-depth analysis of the customer service function. Processes and skills were redesigned and implemented. Customer service representatives were empowered to commit the company's operations resources to solve satisfaction issues. Customers were given the opportunity to call the local company outlet directly and to ask questions, let off steam, complain, get product support, resolve problems, or access additional services. It worked. Customer defections were cut in half. Profitability returned.
>
> The strong customer service function also helped to cultivate and grow relationships with customers. Customer service representatives would regularly call customers to express appreciation for their business, or to ask if further services could be extended to them.

Linking the messages of all functions of the selling organization that have either direct or indirect contact with customers is critical to providing a consistent value message to the customer. We want to have our customer comfortable knowing that in our organization the right hand does know what the left is doing. A goal of coordinating the messages is to never have a customer ask, "Do you people talk to each other?"

Chapter Summary

It is important to link changes made within a selling organization with marketing and customer service functions. Marketing and customer service can make or break the value created for and delivered to customers. Messages delivered to customers should be clear, concise, and linked within all company operations so that customers have a seamless, non-contradictory experience.

8

Transform Your Culture: A Case Study

...and the true romance which the world exists to realize, will be the transformation of genius into practical power.

—Ralph Waldo Emerson

The sales management team also can benefit from project management principles that we established in Chapter 6 were so important for customer teams.

Studies of what motivates people at work have shown time and again that people get the biggest motivations to work hard from a sense of competence—of knowing that they are good at something and can achieve gratifying results from it. Sales leaders can tap into this powerful motivator by putting in place the simple directions, processes, and supports that will encourage selling organization members to move with confidence and competence toward their goals, one small step at a time.

One of the most exceptional and gifted leaders with whom we have worked in a number of his sales leadership positions over the years gives us an excellent example of leading his team. In all of these assignments he has demonstrated excellent sales leadership practices. Here is what he did in one such role to promote culture change in a large complex sales organization.

> When Adam became sales vice president of a large technology company, he set out to talk to many of his team's most important and influential customers. Although he was not expecting to hear a chorus of praise for his sales team, he was somewhat rattled by how negative the

96

customers were, and these were customers who were heavily invested in the firm. Adam saw at once that his team was failing to provide basic account management support for these priority customers.

The feedback told him the teams were devoting all their time to individual opportunities and deals, and were not engaging with customers on business issues meaningful to them. The company had a practice of assigning several people, each with a specific product focus, to a particular opportunity, which forced customers to try to put together their own solutions. Adam believed it was actually undermining the development of meaningful business relationships founded on solutions and trust.

Adam knew that the problems he faced with his team were not the result of errors by his predecessor or ineptitude on the part of his team; they were the result of too many "good" years. However, the business environment had changed dramatically, and it was obvious that old ways were not working. Adam took a hard look at the most painful problems and identified five critical needs that had to be addressed.

1. Define a meaningful account management methodology

2. Facilitate resource management for optimum performance

3. Establish a team approach to selling

4. Elevate thinking about the customer above product sales

5. Get people to do the right things

Adam knew that just defining the strategic issues would not be enough to develop an organization that delivered value to customers. He realized that he had to essentially retool his organization, and that doing so would be a challenge. It meant he had to win the hearts and minds of his management team, account executives, and their teams. He had to firmly ground them in some fundamentals, patiently guide them every step of the way, and ask them to be accountable for results. What he had to do, in short, was to rebuild the team from the inside out—focused on delivering customer value.

Going Live

In the quarter before the start of the company's fiscal year, CPS assisted Adam in designing and facilitating a planning session with his seven executives. He wanted to get agreement on where they were as a selling organization, and where they wanted to go. The outcome would be a project plan for what they had to do to get there.

They examined their goals, strategies, and work plans. They looked at what was wrong, and what they needed to do better. Out of this session came a list of four strategy initiatives that they individually and collectively were committed to supporting.

1. Solutions growth
2. Team communications
3. Investing in human capital
4. A value scorecard

This group was tasked with driving the initiatives, and a project head was assigned to be responsible for each initiative. Adam knew that these initiatives were, in fact, his sales agenda.

Next, he scheduled a planning workshop for the management team, which included 40 managers at all levels. In this session, first-level managers were asked to link their objectives to the selling organization's four initiatives, identify what parts of their own responsibilities would help to drive the agenda, and then identify and articulate personal actions to move the agenda forward.

What Adam was doing was cascading accountability to the first-level team. The next thing they would have to do is assess and align their salespeople with these objectives and actions plans. Adam had several objectives of his own in conducting this session.

- Instill best-practices processes supportive of customer value and growth
- Develop and grow the sales management team
- Establish a discipline that would cascade these best practices throughout the whole selling organization
- Establish accountability for making this happen with each individual salesperson in the company

Cascading the Process and Enrolling the Team

First, they assembled in breakout groups to identify issues facing the sales organization in general and key objectives related to those issues. There were a number of barriers, including the following ones.

- Shrinking information technology budgets
- Account managers spend too much time with critical situations, administration, and maintenance concerns

- Account managers need better skills for making effective executive calls
- Business solution value needs to be better understood before negotiation
- Contract terms and conditions negotiating too slow
- Inability to track total cost of sale and sales call usage by representative or opportunity

Some strategic imperatives began to surface.

- Better customer segmentation
- Expand distribution channel options
- Improve sales/technical communications
- Explore timeline/checklist process for stages in sales process
- Move from account manager and product-centric model to a team-selling model
- Improve ability to measure account profitability

After the general brainstorming sessions, the group framed these objectives in the context of four key initiatives (growth, communication, human capital, value scorecard) identified months earlier by their second-level superiors. Under each of these they listed about a dozen hard recommendations.

Adam's sense was that his sales organization's development of human capital needed particular focus. Could our people pull this off? What could we do to help them? For this, Adam developed a "Boston box" matrix for identifying a salesperson's maturity in both *getting it done* and *doing it right*. Getting it done means closing sales and making the numbers. However, this can be done in some cases at the cost of alienating or losing customers over the long term and/or alienating people internally within the sales organization.

Doing it right is the complementary dimension of getting it done. It means being open to all possibilities, cultivating good customer relationships, going the extra mile, generally having a wide view of value creation for the customer, and operating within the governance of the customer rules of engagement.

In a follow-on meeting with his entire sales management team, Adam asked participants to identify characteristics of a salesperson in each quadrant. The headings at the top of each quadrant indicate the appropriate management action toward the individual with those characteristics.

Characteristics of Sales Performance

GETTING IT DONE	Coach/Teach	Reward
	<u>Coach/Teach</u> • Meet revenue targets • Limited scope • Low customer satisfaction • Heavy support need • Reluctant to utilize sales tools • Meet deadlines • Luck out • Discount too much	<u>Reward</u> • Effective prospecting • Meet revenue target with best-practice standards • High customer satisfaction across entire enterprise • New products • Profitable • Reference ability • Complete solution • Trusted advisors/resource
	<u>Motivate/Remove</u> • No prospecting • No revenue • Low customer satisfaction with lack of commitment • Ignore teams • Miss deadlines • Poor time management • Lack motivation	<u>Coach/Motivate</u> • Regular prospecting with limited sources • Limited revenue with best practice standards • Monitor customer satisfaction with building enterprise • Mentoring

DOING IT RIGHT

This is the beginning of first-level management accountability for developing people. Managers at each level assess the behavior and results of their subordinates.

After these two sessions, the four initiative owners had milestone-based project plans to guide and measure their progress. These plans were part of Adam's communications strategy for cultural change. The team leaders for the four initiatives reported results of their progress every month.

Valuing People

This brings us to a critical part of any plan for major change, and especially any plan to introduce and enforce accountability in selling organizations. Targeted initiatives need to be anchored at the most basic level of all organizations—the individual. Each person is the source of the organization's collective strength, and a resource that merits its greatest care and attention.

In a knowledge economy, many people are seeking ways to increase their own personal value through their work. They are seeking validation of their competence, improvement of their skills set, a record of achievement, and confirmation of their worth as a valued employee. Good people need to feel challenged and believe that there is an opportunity to grow.

The other side of that coin is that if someone's personal capital is not growing and gaining worth, then they can withdraw their services from the company. They either quit producing or they leave.

What this human capital exercise did for the participants was to create excitement around the selling organization's potential to succeed, and their own competence in helping that to happen. It invited them to explore the possibilities for improvement, gave them a large goal for which to strive, and set out a clear path to achieve it. Here are some of their comments after the brainstorming and planning sessions.

- We came up with a radical initiative. If we follow through, there is a high probability of achieving our plan.

- I am energized because this is "our" initiative, and when we go back it will be well received up and down the organization. However, we must be consistent on focus and resist outside distractions.

- Will we make the numbers? I cannot see it right now. But I can see us being a very successful, highly efficient, top-notch, enthusiastic sales organization. The attitude of the people is absolutely critical. We need to have meetings like this to openly discuss issues so we can provide effective leadership to the organization.

- I liked the solution we created here. If we are allowed to do what we committed to, we will be successful. Still cannot see the number, but see removing obstacles.

- We have a much better feeling of the pain in the field caused by many corporate initiatives.

- We are in a much better position to communicate "most important" and how we can help the field in their mission.

- I am not comfortable yet that we can attain the number, but this is doable and we can attain results.

See how the group became energized with possibilities? Ongoing open communication regarding progress gets traction and momentum behind key organizational change initiatives. Due to the effective foundation built by Adam and his management team, the behavior changed throughout the organization in a way that enabled business to grow in the most tumultuous of industry segments.

Chapter Summary

As mentioned earlier, the CSO must clearly articulate his vision and expectations for transforming his organization. He must enroll his management team in the initiative, asking them to identify high-impact initiatives for advancing the transformation. To succeed, the initiatives must be managed like a project, with accountability cascading through the organization to the salespeople at the customer-facing level.

PART 3.
STRENGTHEN THE SALES CULTURE

CHAPTER 9.
ACCOUNT MANAGEMENT EXECUTION
CHAPTER 10.
THE CASE FOR RELATIONSHIP INVESTMENTS
CHAPTER 11.
LEVERAGE RELATIONSHIP INVESTMENTS

How do sales executives create a culture of personal accountability and solid execution in their selling teams? Great sales executives know that they must instill a repeatable discipline for those they lead. This discipline can be used at levels throughout the customer-facing team to deliver value to the customer and results to the business.

It is our experience that great sales executives develop personal leadership skills over time through openness to new models, ideas, and approaches that can be tuned for their particular situation. Earlier, we introduced the chief sales officer agenda, which many great sales leaders have used to identify major structural barriers that must be addressed to ensure sustainable and profitable growth.

In this section, we will introduce a complementary model focused specifically on account management execution. It provides another thoughtful framework to pinpoint critical elements that your team must implement in order to deliver maximum value to your customers and to your company. We will also explore the *relationship glue* that holds it all together.

9

Account Management Execution

Leadership without the discipline of execution is incomplete and ineffective.

—*Larry Bossidy and Ram Charan,*
in Execution: The Discipline of Getting Things Done

In Part 1, we introduced the chief sales officer agenda, and we established that account management execution was at the top of the *must-do* list. In Part 2, we established that account management execution is especially critical for the most important customers. They deserve and demand it. Now, we will spend some time delving into what account management execution is.

How is the sales organization perceived in your enterprise? Is it seen as a necessary evil in dealing with demanding customers or is it viewed as a critical business function in fulfilling the company's go-to-market strategy? In many organizations, the sales function is not viewed with the same respect as are finance, product development, service delivery, or human resources. How would the votes be cast when assessing the effectiveness of your selling team in delivering revenue and value?

Much of how a sales organization is perceived derives from how it functions. Is the sales organization primarily occupied with managing complaints and fighting customer-related fires? If so, the sales function may be seen as a group of expensive customer care representatives who spend their time in task force meetings instead of selling. Or, is the sales team viewed as a bunch of professional schmoozers who spend too much time inviting prospects to attend any number of corporate-sponsored events?

No matter what the current view, the more important question becomes, "How do sales leaders guide the selling organization in managing accounts to ensure that a balanced approach is taken to drive revenue, build relationships with customers, and address customers' ongoing satisfaction?" If a CSO envisions and positions the selling organization as the point of a spear that can be directed at targets of value, then the selling team will stand a better chance of being viewed as a strategic weapon of the company's success. This discipline will help convince company leadership to invest in sales, and more importantly, help the company deliver on its value promise to its most important customers.

No one is confused with the selling organization's importance in driving revenue. What is less clear to many is the role of outstanding account management execution in a selling team's ability to drive sustainable results for their company while delivering extraordinary value to the customer. Flawless execution of account strategies and initiatives is what separates great companies from mediocre companies. If account management is not a priority for a company, then long-term profitable growth is an elusive dream. We strongly advise sales leaders to treat account management in a deliberate and purposeful fashion.

Good account management execution in a selling organization can create a powerful bridge between account representatives and the strategy and revenue expectations of the company. Now more than ever, companies need to make account management a key part of the selling organization's discipline and the company's business.

Account Management Definition

Account management encompasses the entire set of interactions between a buyer and a seller, from the onset of the commercial relationship through the purchase and resulting use of goods or services. Included in the spectrum are communication, relationship development, fulfillment, and ongoing support. There are a number of important components that are essential for successful account management. Representative elements include information gathering, strategizing, account planning, relationship-building, team development, and assigning accountabilities for strategic as well as day-to-day transactions. All these elements work to activate a business-to-business strategy at the account level that will produce the highest value recognition and the greatest breakthrough results for both the buyer and seller.

The complexity and magnitude of great account management is often underestimated. In fact, when investigating the top priorities of sales leaders during our CSO agenda research, we found that the most commonly listed area of dissatisfaction or concern was account management execution. Our discussions highlighted the large number of variables and organizational functions beyond the CSO's span of control that impact sales' ability to deliver outstanding business-to-business revenue performance.

The structure of today's organizations often makes it necessary for selling organizations to operate in a matrixed manner. The challenges associated with allocating resources appropriately to address individual opportunities, specific client relationships, and product or service expertise frequently result in a customer-facing team that blends sales and non-sales personnel. To ensure consistency, accountability, and results, a well-defined and holistic strategy for executing account management must be in place.

The Account Management Execution (AME) Model

CPS developed the CSO agenda to help sales leaders see and understand the range of critical and interrelated competencies that need to be in place to shape a successful selling organization. From this outline of key competencies, CSOs and their managers could select a manageable number of initiatives to work on over the year, according to their priorities.

After the agenda had been used by a large number of CPS clients over the ensuing years, CPS conducted additional research to understand where the agenda was being used most effectively and what benefits were being realized, and to identify which of the activities in the agenda was most important for sales organizations using the model. We wanted to identify the key success factors and initiatives engaged by high-level sales executives in support of their direct sales teams and their most important customers. Sales executives from a range of complex companies were interviewed, including the CSOs of Oracle, Microsoft, Perot Systems, and Martin Marietta.

As highlighted previously, this representative group of senior sales executives unanimously identified account management execution as the most critical initiative requiring focus, energy, and investment of resources. The top priority for almost half of the respondents (and one of the top five for all CSOs) was ensuring delivery and recognition of client value by developing and executing on customer plans.

These CSOs recognized that the discipline of managing their most important or strategic accounts could be the fundamental differentiator in growing top-line revenue. In a time of fierce competition, most sales organizations need to fight for some kind of differentiation from rivals. Customers are telling many sales organizations that they judge their suppliers on how those sales teams execute and manage these business relationships.

What was needed, we realized, was a new model for account management execution that sales leaders could use to identify gaps in critical account functions, and to crystallize what they most needed to work on. To this end, the AME model was developed.

We define account management execution as the discipline, or *how*, of the activities and competencies required to influence and support the customer. It often includes the tools and infrastructure to prepare for and support the development and delivery of account management activities.

Like the CSO model, the AME model presents a set of critical activities that are the building blocks of solid and successful account management execution. All or at least most of these exist in most organizations. However, these activities may not be optimized, either individually or as a whole. Also like the CSO model, the AME model is useful to the selling organization to the extent that its components are made actionable in the organization.

The more a company's success is dictated by its relationships with a short list of accounts, the more important account management execution is. Most people have heard of the 80/20 rule. One of our customers has revenue-generation programs that are 90 percent focused on only two percent of its customer base. For them, account management execution is critical. The AME model follows.

Account Management Execution Model

© 2002 by Critical Path Strategies, Inc. All Rights Reserved.

The AME Model

The AME model is structured in five levels, representing major areas of competence.

The bottom two levels are foundational levels.

1. Defining the strategic account management model

2. Deploying the strategic account management program

Activities in these levels are largely undertaken by sales executives and, to the extent that is required, by organization executives. They are critical foundational steps. Without these, the sales organization cannot deliver client value.

The top three levels are customer-facing and execution-related.

3. Ensuring client alignment

4. Developing and executing the plan

5. Demonstrating value

These affect everyone in the sales organization and its customers. These three areas of activity are the action levels that are everyone's responsibility. Each level has multiple elements, for a total of 15 key elements that the organization needs to address.

The CSO needs to work on the foundation levels; they define how the sales organization is going to work. Essentially, what the CSO comes up with for these foundation activities needs to be designed into the sales organization. When this happens, the selling organization is able to concentrate on the top three levels, where the crucial customer-facing action takes place and the money is made. The rest of this chapter further explains these levels of activity.

Level 1. Defining the Strategic Account Management Model

Selling Process Definition	Selling Organization	People and Incentives	Infrastructure	Corporate Alignment

This level addresses the underlying structure of the AME model. Specifically, it concerns the process, organization, compensation system, infrastructure, and alignment of the AME model with company strategy and values. The five elements of this level are discussed below.

Selling process definition. This element addresses the sales process, which we discussed in Part 2. It refers to the design of a documented, scalable, repeatable process that is used to support a company's strategic accounts.

As we said earlier, the sales process is the selling organization's backbone. It facilitates everyone's job by making the best use of resources, at the right times, for the right purposes. Following a sales process that is clear to all salespeople increases the velocity of pipeline projects and focuses efforts where they will do the most good.

Selling organization. This foundation element concerns the design of a resource deployment process for all customer contact functions. At this point, sales leaders determine how many accounts they will administer as platinum service, whether they are going to have two or three tiers of accounts, what channels they will use for what purposes, and what proportion of direct relationships they will engage. It is an organization, or organizing function, which most sales groups undertake yearly to ensure smooth progress toward goals.

People and incentives. As we have said, if you have a big disconnect between what you want people to do and how you reward them, they will likely go in directions that get them to their goals but not necessarily yours. This element of the foundation reminds you to take some care in designing the compensation plan and incentives for the strategic account management team. Will there be performance-based compensation? Commissions? Will people be rewarded on the basis of the whole company's performance? The design of these systems will point the selling team in the right direction with their wallet as their compass.

Infrastructure. A modest percentage of the sales team will have natural sales talents. They are *unconscious competents* who are outstanding performers without knowing why. The majority, however, are not, and will benefit from whatever tools and support the sales organization can provide. These performance support tools include systems and operational processes. Examples are contact management applications, automated proposal generators, work order processes and change protocols, marketing collateral in support of sales, and reporting procedures.

Corporate alignment. We hear a lot about alignment these days; for example, alignment of business objectives and information technology strategies. We believe it is even more important to ensure that the goals of the strategic account management selling teams (and their approach to supporting strategic customers) are aligned with the company's corporate values and goals.

Not only do salespeople need to be aware of and promote new product offerings from lines of business, but they must also ensure that the intangible value associated with an offering is promoted—and recognized—in strategic accounts. Also, if the salespeople are the company's eyes and ears in the marketplace, they are also the best representatives of the company's core values.

They are the voice of the corporate vision. For example, if research and development leadership is a core value, why would sales teams not align that leadership with the research needs of their most important customers?

Level 2. Deploying the Strategic Account Management Program

Account Selection	Team Resource Deployment	Account Management Methodology	Account Management Discipline

This section of the model focuses on deployment of the strategic account program. It includes the process for selecting accounts for the program, teaming, and account management methodology and management approach. This is the next step in making the selling organization ready for targeted, productive action.

Account selection. Here is where the sales leadership identifies the top, most-valued strategic accounts, let us say the top 25 of a total of 3,000 accounts. The criteria for account selection and prioritization will be particular to each organization, but no one can ignore percentage of revenue from an account as a key criterion. Other factors might include level of complexity (number of lines of business), global reach (for greater selling opportunities), degree of current penetration, and leadership in their industry.

Team resources deployment. This activity is about getting the right people to the right clients and opportunities. Astute sales leaders will always try to match the best skills to the tasks for which they are most appropriate.

We discussed this idea earlier when we talked about knowing your people, and suggested that those with special talents should be directed and encouraged to use these skills in their daily responsibilities as part of sales teams. Alternatively, sales leaders may choose to place individuals with a nascent spark of a special skill in roles where this skill can be developed and flourish. In the right context and with the right customer, this person can gain confidence to let his particular talent shine.

Account management methodology. This refers to definition of the processes and toolsets used to develop strategies and plans for strategic accounts. There are many methodologies currently available, including the critical path methodology of CPS. Each selling organization needs to carefully consider what kind of approach is best for its own circumstances and resources—what it can manage to do. The important thing is to adopt a methodology, adapt it to your business, and use it!

Account management discipline. We identified this feature as a key foundation element of account management planning because we believe it to be central to any hopes of sales success. As we noted earlier, we consider it to be a key differentiator among sales organizations. It is the discipline of sales management to participate in the sales team's progress, through regular reviews, coaching, incentives, demands for accountability, and running interference when needed. Management's active role in supporting customer-facing teams is what distinguishes an extraordinary selling organization.

Level 3. Ensuring Client Alignment

Client Goal Alignment	Client Process Integration	Team and Client Communication

One of the overwhelmingly dominant characteristics found in high-performance strategic account teams is their almost innate ability to align and model their business to create value with their client's goals and needs. We have found that this ability can be developed, learned, supported, and institutionalized with a high degree of success.

This part of the model relates to implementation of methods, tools, and procedures to align and communicate with clients. There are just three elements here, but they are correspondingly more critical for successful account management execution.

Client goal alignment. Every sales organization reaching for success must ensure that the account team's goals are clearly aligned with the strategic client's goals. It may sound obvious, but it is not always practiced. Without doing this, the sales team is just *making numbers* and more often than not turns out to be a one-shot wonder.

For these accounts especially, the sales team needs to articulate the benefits to be derived by the client when the sales team achieves its own goals for that client. We cannot stress this enough. It just will not work without sales teams constantly revalidating the value they are delivering to customers.

Client process integration. Every client organization has its own set of business processes. The selling organization needs to structure its own selling processes with a particular client to match the client's way of doing business. Notwithstanding its own sales process, the selling organization must map to the client's business model.

For example, Proctor and Gamble reengineered how they do business to accommodate the way Wal-Mart does business. What it meant for Proctor and Gamble was that consumers now buy more than 40 percent of Proctor and Gamble consumer products through Wal-Mart. Another example of integration might include sales personnel embedded in the client's organization to manage key aspects of the sales development and delivery function. It is a great testament to many of our clients to see themselves drawn into a customer's organization chart.

Team and client communication. As every project manager knows, one of the critical determinants of project success is clear, regular, and open communication among project team members, and between the team and sponsors. Well-functioning sales teams are characterized by the same high level of communication among team members and, especially important for them, with the client organization.

Ideally, the sales teams are *zippered* with their client organization counterparts. (We will develop this theme in Chapter 11.) However, both sales and client organization people can usefully manage different parts of multiple projects when there is frequent updating of the status of the initiatives, resource adjustments, and always a clear focus on benefits for both parties.

Level 4. Developing and Executing the Plan

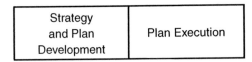

The fourth level begins the execution part of the model, and deals with best practices in strategy and plan development processes for executing strategies and plans for priority customers. Once the selling organization has achieved the best possible degree of alignment with the client, the next issue to address is, "How do we accomplish what we want to do?"

Strategy and plan development. A sharp selling organization has a defined, repeatable process to develop a strategy and an action plan to address each client's key initiatives. The plan is the selling team's *critical path* to achieving its goals—by achieving the client's goals. It enables the selling team to balance making quota today with being successful in the future on a sustainable basis.

The selling team's plan for each client needs to include account strategy, account planning, relationship strategy, sales opportunity strategies, work plans, and call preparation. Sales leaders and teams should apply an efficient, self-documenting project management discipline to the development and management of these strategies, which need to be understood by everyone on the team, and the customer.

- **Goal**. Results desired for customer and seller
- **Milestones**. The what, when, and who needed to at least barely achieve the goal
- **Best next actions**. The what, when, and who needed to keep momentum behind each milestone
- **Project management**. Who owns the project, and how will accountability be managed

Plan execution. This part of the model involves making the best use of resources to achieve the greatest results. It means day-to-day resource deployment to advance best next actions on each milestone of the plan. Solid plan execution not only makes teams perform better and raises their morale, but also glues them more firmly to customer needs.

Results. One of our customers measures employee morale and customer satisfaction yearly. He found that employee morale results had a high correlation with customer satisfaction results (both poor or both good). He observed that satisfied customers generated 20 percent more sales, 30 percent more profit, and significantly higher retention rates than those with low satisfaction ratings. Correspondingly, these customer-facing teams loved their jobs and were engaged with enthusiasm.

Level 5. Demonstrating Value

| Value Creation |
| and Recognition |

Appropriately, we place the customer at the top of the model. It is at this level that customers recognize the value they receive from selling team efforts. Demonstrating value involves articulating the business impact account management execution delivers.

Whether the selling organization is responding to a customer problem, developing and executing sales and account strategies, preparing for and executing a sales call, or delivering and implementing products and services, all customer-facing teams need to constantly step back from internal issues and demands and *wrap themselves around the customer.*

Here is where the power of the sales agenda and the sales process really comes into play, by successfully demonstrating what value means.

- Jointly measuring the delivery of results to the customer's business
- Jointly celebrating the achievement of value creation
- Confirming that the aligned team is positioned to deliver even more value in the future

The pinnacle of the AME model pyramid, and the point of all the topics in this book, is for the selling organization to *demonstrate value at every point of contact with the customer.*

Just as the CSO model does for sales management, the AME model outlines the activities that are critical for account management success. Its elements are the embodiment of the phrase: *It is all about the customer.*

Validation of the AME Model

The Strategic Account Management Association (SAMA) is an association comprising representatives of 2,000 corporate selling organizations. In 2003, SAMA engaged CPS to use our AME model to survey a wide spectrum of sales professionals. Participants were asked to complete a Web-based assessment of their account management execution practices for their company's most important customers.

The assessment was intended for sales leaders seeking to understand best practices in managing customer-facing teams in strategic accounts, and their companies' position vis-à-vis best practices. It was also meant to help them drive extraordinary results in their most important accounts.

A broad range of industries was represented, with a majority in the Industrial (29 percent) and Information Technology (16 percent) sectors. The remaining respondents were primarily from Consulting (12 percent) or other Service (12 percent) industries. The largest proportion (40 percent) comprised respondents in companies with fewer than 1,000 employees. Most respondents (65 percent) held a middle management or an executive management position.

By the time this analysis was carried out, 126 respondents had completed the assessment. While these self-assessments of the first set of respondents cannot be independently verified, there does appear to be a good demographic mix that allows preliminary analysis. As we continue the research, we are finding no fatal flaws.

Research Findings

In general, there was a very high level of correlation between how respondents rated their strategic account program at any level of the AME model and their overall account management execution assessment rating. Consistent performance, it appears, is consistently rewarded. There is no indication that respondents could skip a level in the model or put less emphasis on the foundational layers and still rate well.

While all program elements had a significant positive relationship to predicting success, a few were stronger predictors.

- The best predictors of success were *value recognition, value delivery, and alignment with the client's goals.* These elements are the traditional mainstays of quality client relationships—providing and communicating value and goal alignment (focusing on the right value to deliver).

- Elements of program documentation also had a strong relationship to both the overall rating and the strategic account measures of success. They included *defining the sales process, deploying the account management methodology, and account strategy and plan development.*

Statistical techniques grouped participants into four performance-based clusters, which represent a set of participants with similar performance ratings.

1. **Investigating.** This group has the lowest level of commitment to or involvement in account management execution.

2. **Focused Performers.** These respondents are executing on a subset of the account management execution elements.

3. **Working At It.** The majority of participants in this group have a strategic account program in place, but without the superior execution demonstrated by the top group.

4. **Stars.** These performers have strategic account programs in place, are executing well, and showing consistent improvement.

The following graph depicts the performance groups' average business success with their strategic accounts. Participants rated their business success with their strategic accounts in terms of customer satisfaction, wallet share, growth, sales, general and administrative expense, and quota attainment. As one would expect, the strategic account success of those Investigating account management execution is relatively low. Stars get a solid payoff from their efforts. The rewards for Focused Performers and those Working At It are remarkably similar. Both of these groups were able to capitalize on their account management efforts.

The scale represents, from the left: (1) strategic accounts never out-perform other accounts, to (5) strategic accounts always outperform others.

AME Performance Groups

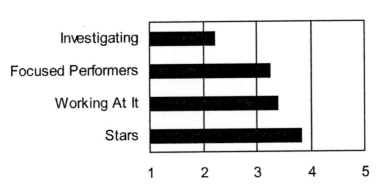

The average scores for each group on each of the 15 AME model elements are depicted in the next graph. Note that the relative rankings of the four performance groups remain consistent across all 15 elements. All four groups show a strong correlation between account management execution program performance rating and strategic account success.

AME Research Findings

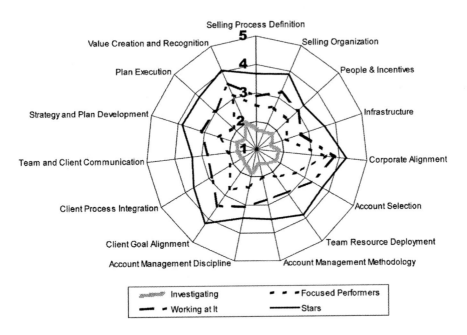

The results clearly show that Stars consistently outperformed the other performance clusters on addressing elements of the AME model. They also had the highest correlation of performance rating to strategic account success. The results for each performance cluster are described in more detail in the next sections.

Investigating. The Investigating group has little focus on account management execution. These respondents frequently did not have a strategic account program. Their interest in taking a 100-plus-question assessment may indicate that they are investigating or pre-assessing their performance on key account management execution elements. Perhaps they are in the program evaluation or baseline stages of strategic account program development. Here are the highlights of results for this group.

Of the Investigating group, 73 percent did not have a strategic account program (compared to 75 percent of all participants). This very large difference came with a hefty penalty in the overall success of their most important accounts, which rarely out-performed other client accounts.

The group's score in strategic account success indicators was significantly below that of other groups. This group had particularly low scores in plan execution, and low scores in aligning to their internal strategies and aligning their goals with their clients' goals. This might be expected for a group that often did not have a strategic account program in place.

Focused Performers. The Focused Performers was the only group that was able to do better on its strategic account success indicators than its overall account management execution rating might have predicted. This group was below average in its overall survey score (2.4 versus the 2.9 average overall) and did not exceed average on any element of the account management execution rating. Yet, they scored themselves close to average on the business success indicators of customer satisfaction, growth, share, expense control, and quota attainment. Here are the key results for Focused Performers.

- They tended to focus on aligning their efforts to internal corporate strategies, aligning goals with their clients' goals, and delivering value. In these performance elements alone, they achieved near-average self-rated success in their strategic accounts.

- They are not focused, however, on the planning elements of account management execution. They have particularly low scores in client plan execution, the client strategy planning process, and the rigor of their account management methodology.

- They rated second lowest on strategic account program measurements, although far more of them have a strategic account program than the Investigating group (65 percent have a program).

Working At It. The Working At It group seems to be about average in almost every respect. Their account management execution performance is slightly above average on every rating element measured. These respondents had the same high and low ratings in their account management execution work as respondents overall. This gives them an average performance rating of 3.2 (as compared to the entire pool's average of 2.9). Their success indicators are just below this, falling almost exactly on average in every case.

This group had the highest percentage of strategic account programs in place but exhibits only average success, perhaps illustrating the difference between having a program versus true excellence in a program.

- They rated high in aligning to their own corporate strategies and value delivery.

- They had a low score, however, in sales tool infrastructure and the rigor of their account management methodology.

- The role of fee-based services at these companies is bi-modal; it is either very important or not offered at all (this was more evenly distributed in other clusters).

Stars. The respondents who rated highest came from a broad spectrum of industries, company sizes, and other demographic characteristics. This is good news, since this indicates that success is not dependent on being big, or being a "solutions" seller. Success is a simple matter of *superior, disciplined execution.*

Stars exceeded the average by the greatest margin in their systematic and long-range view on deployment of client teams and relationship executives. This was part of a strong overall account management execution effort with all elements scoring well above the lower levels achieved by other clusters. How did the Stars rate themselves?

- Star respondents rated themselves highest in account management execution elements overall.

- They rated themselves as the most successful in their strategic account results, surpassing the results of the rest of their company's customers.

- The Stars scored themselves very high on aligning their programs to their companies' strategies and aligning goals with their clients.

- They also reported a high rating on delivering value to customers and having this value recognized by customers.

Stars tended to be higher-level executives than average and controlled a larger percentage of their sales representatives—about 70 percent versus an average span of control of 40 percent represented in the rest of the clusters.

Summary. These results show that making an investment in sound best practices, good methodology, and a well-executed strategic account program will positively impact companies' attainment of quota, customer satisfaction, share, and growth. According to this analysis, the level of execution on account management execution elements is a reliable indicator of the success of strategic accounts. Findings are summarized in the following table.

Summary Findings of AME Performance Groups

	Investigating	Focused Performers	Working At It	Stars
Focus	Frequently did not have a strategic account management program	Align account management execution efforts to corporate strategies and align with customer goals	Work on all elements of account management execution	Invest in sound best practices, good methodology, and strategic account management program
Industry	Most do not offer fee services	Most from smaller companies	Cross industry Broad sizes	Higher percentage of Services or Consulting industries
Key Findings	Little difference in performance of most important accounts versus all accounts Low in aligning their internal strategies with their clients' strategies	Little focus on planning, plan execution, and process rigor Approach often results in higher attainment of strategic account management	Low in sales tool infrastructure Low in planning rigor	Respondents seem to have the ability to implement corrective action Results in strategic account management program higher than in other accounts

Additional assessments may reveal more about this phenomenon. Our hypothesis is that inconsistent performance of account management execution best practices will not result in anything beyond average success. The example of the Stars can serve as a useful guideline for those seeking extraordinary sales.

Using the Model

Like the CSO model, the AME model lays out a super-set of factors that all have an important bearing on successfully managing major accounts. Also like the CSO model, the AME model offers an opportunity for sales leaders to identify a small number of factors on which to concentrate selling organization efforts, in a general way, to improve sales execution across all accounts. It provides an important way to assess the status of account management *performance* in the selling organization, as shown in the account management execution assessment findings.

Using the AME model to best advantage follows the pattern of suggestions for using the CSO agenda, outlined in Part 2.

- **Identify a few areas of activity to improve.** For example, if an assessment reveals that a high proportion of engagements falter at a particular selling stage, the selling organization would be well-served to focus the efforts of the sales organization—at all levels—to redress this problem. Some of our clients ask us to do an assessment we call sales process optimization.

- **Lay out a strategic plan for improving the selected areas of activity.** If sales leaders leave improvement to chance, performance will only improve by chance. Selection should be based on reward to the firm and ability to execute.

- **Focus on improvement areas at every level of the selling organization.** This frequently falls into what we call the roles and responsibilities assessment. It examines the question, "What do we and our clients expect from our people and how do we help them fulfill those needs?"

- **Take focused actions to drive improvement and maintain momentum.** At every stage in the sales process, in every encounter between salespeople and sales leaders, and at every point of contact with customers, sales leaders need to ensure that the right actions are being taken to achieve the right outcomes. Start by talking to customers.

We have seen many examples of extraordinary sales and turnarounds from this kind of intentional improvement effort around account management execution. What happens is that the selling organization is naturally raised to a higher level of performance—in many cases, within a year!

It is because some kind of important behavior change has occurred, and not just in the selling organization. When other important non-sales participants (whose support and resources are crucial to the selling effort) see that good use is being made of their investment (dollars and time), they are more likely to get behind the account management efforts of the selling organization. This collaboration means better results for sales leaders, and greater credibility for the selling organization.

The Model in Practice

A model is good for organizing one's efforts, but experience with the model demonstrates how successfully the AME model works in practice. Here are two examples of putting the AME model into practice that brought extraordinary results for a couple of insightful, practical, and disciplined sales leaders.

The Software Company Experience

TSC is a multinational software company, offering increasingly complex solutions to meet its customers' technology needs. Over the course of the 1990s, the company experienced explosive growth through acquisitions, which brought together a wide variety of selling cultures and business processes. By the end of the decade, TSC's 1990s business model created execution challenges at all customer contact points.

There were multiple sales representatives, each aligned with separate product lines, on each account. These sales silos led to inconsistent value propositions presented to customers and prospects. Customers were confused; return on sales went negative. Something had to change.

Through the board of advisors, TSC's customers asked TSC to build long-term, broad relationships with them based on the following needs.

- Align your goals with ours
- Understand our environment
- Tell us what our peers are doing
- Provide information up, down, and across your organization
- Make it more convenient to do business with you

- Elevate the relationship or become a commodity
- Sell tools in unique, packaged offerings
- Teach us how to leverage your technology in our environment
- Help us understand your billing and invoice process

The company realized that although it had a strong presence in the technical community, it needed stronger relationships to provide customers with total enterprise solutions. What they desperately needed was a consistent set of processes for systematic delivery of value in the manner each customer segment needed it.

That meant significant adjustments to the selling organization itself. TSC considered some alternative distribution strategies to meet the concerns of its customer segments. Doing nothing differently would only increase customer confusion and decrease margins. Relying on original equipment manufacturers would leave OEMs responsible for thought leadership.

Outsourcing selling to channels might forfeit customer intimacy, but customers were telling TSC that intimacy is exactly what they wanted. TSC decided to focus on becoming a trusted advisor for systems management issues for its most important customers. They adopted the AME model.

Defining the Model

There was an important feature of TSC's decision that made its use of the model workable and successful. John, vice president of sales, realized that the selling organization had to focus on the people who would be working with the new methodology. John needed to activate the AME model in a way that focused on how salespeople were going to perform in this new environment.

John developed an organization structure that defined the kinds of coverage planned for targeted accounts, and the new kinds of client-facing roles that would facilitate a broader, solution-based relationship with customers.

Challenges and Solutions

TSC faced an array of challenges in refocusing its selling organization. It needed a workable account management methodology, an approach to efficiently deploy resources consistent with the methodology, and a plan and a way to execute it successfully. The following table summarizes TSC's challenges and the solutions they adopted.

Sales Growth Methodology

Account Management Methodology	Team Resource Deployment	Strategy/Plan Development and Plan Execution
CHALLENGE	CHALLENGE	CHALLENGE
Develop methodology that fits the company and field deployment strategy of collaborative teams	Develop approach to efficiently engage all TSC resources	Establish account manager behavior to effectively: • Engage high-level customers in business issue discussions • Build a bridge between customer business problems and TSC offerings
SOLUTION	SOLUTION	SOLUTION
• Scalable methodology to be used effectively for each tier of accounts • Process to facilitate bringing team members into context quickly • Straightforward approach to be basis for TSC's sales management discipline	• Align customer business needs with extended TSC team capabilities • Help team members understand roles and responsibilities • Support and simplify project management	• Leverage CPS strategic account management approach to drive pre-engagement research • Consistently use CPS call plan tool • Develop account, opportunity and relationship plans, and monitor resulting critical path action plans

Results

Much of the work of revitalizing TSC's selling organization through a total enterprise account management program has been successfully undertaken, and refinements are continually underway. The results of this realigned, customer-focused initiative are already gratifying. After a year, the TSC sales organization reduced its sales expense-to-revenue ratio by 20 percent and maintained share of wallet of its customers in turbulent economic times.

It is a simple plan: Maintain customer focus in everything the TSC selling organization does. However, it is not necessarily easy. It is taking a lot of effort on everyone's part, a great deal of understanding, commitment, and sheer energy from everyone—salespeople and sales leaders alike.

Think of the effort involved to retool how over 400 sales team members work, and the patience and persistence that requires. John and his salespeople deserve much well-earned credit for their vision and execution. These are the things they realized.

- People are the heart and soul of a sales organization and its key to success.
- People deserve to be treated with dignity and understanding.
- Focus on the customer is the only thing that matters.
- Customer focus must be paired with accountability.
- Persistence and patience are necessary when undertaking major change.

TSC's vice president of sales believes that applying discipline to account management execution allowed the company to position itself as a thought leader in business solutions. The development and execution of an overall account strategy led to some of the most significant growth TSC ever experienced—after the growth that caused the problem of sales silos in the first place! More importantly, it enabled the company to move systematically from salesmanship to added strength on the basis of a consistent, repeatable, workable account management execution process.

The following client story is a good example of how, for many sales organizations in today's business environment, there is little alternative but to grab the challenge head-on and make account management execution a priority in the selling organization.

Manufacturing Solutions Corporation

A Transformation in Progress

Manufacturing Solutions Corporation (MSC) is known as "the tool man of the hard goods manufacturing industry." For light and heavy manufacturing alike, MSC offers a wide variety of products and technology, ranging from parts to motors to complete sub-assemblies. The company also operates hundreds of distribution service centers worldwide that sell equipment and parts. From commodities to OEM parts and spares, MSC wants to supply what its manufacturing customers need.

In a few short years, MSC expanded from a well-known and respected niche parts supplier to a technology leader supplying integrated systems. This explosive growth, fueled by over 50 strategic acquisitions during the last 10 years, brought together a wide variety of selling cultures and business processes, as well as a portfolio of hundreds of products.

The acquisitions occurred so quickly that internal decision-making became increasingly complicated. The leaders of acquired companies were accustomed to running their businesses autonomously and were reluctant to relinquish their personal authority. Not unexpectedly, the resulting sales silos led to confused customers who were not really sure who was going to call on them and what the value proposition of the day would be.

In individual conversations and written surveys, MSC's customers voiced their concern. While MSC's acquisitions had broadened the product lines to provide an end-to-end solution, the customers were irritated by the resulting multi-legged sales calls. Did it really take four or five MSC sales representatives to represent the entire product line?

To the customers, MSC had too many interfaces. They wanted a company that was easy to do business with. Here is what they told MSC.

- Deliver on time
- Supply products that work
- Provide quality service
- Keep price consistent with quality
- Honor commitments
- Respond with appropriate urgency
- Work with us to resolve problems
- Prevent surprises
- Make it easy to do business with you

A Management Summit

Bob Nelson, the chief operating officer, decided something had to change. He assembled his management team for a series of intensely focused meetings to develop a strategy that would enable the company to balance plans for continued growth through acquisitions with a scalable infrastructure. Conferring with industry leaders and management experts, MSC leadership acknowledged that in order to achieve a single face to the customer, the executive team needed to create a new culture founded on providing value to the customer on a consistent basis.

This new culture had to be grounded in processes and infrastructure that made doing business with MSC easy, and supported unerring quality at each point of customer contact. The management team identified seven core processes to implement on a company-wide basis, and named a manager accountable for each process. The team decided to tackle the order acquisition/customer retention process first. Charlie Davis, an executive new to MSC, was assigned ownership of this critical process.

Charlie joined MSC after a merger between his company and MSC. His company, a leading supplier of parts to the automotive industry, operated primarily in the Great Lakes region. Charlie was no stranger to running a successful business. He led his company for nearly two decades, growing sales 20 percent per year.

Charlie learned early in his career the harsh realities of leading a distribution company. He realized that the only true differentiation between what he offered versus his competitors was customer service. He built a company driven by focused sales and marketing that promised and delivered better customer service than could be provided by other larger competitors. It was this experience that shaped the management philosophy he would apply in developing and deploying a customer-driven order acquisition/customer retention process at MSC.

Defining the Sales Agenda—TEAM

Charlie wanted to create an approach to MSC's key customers that leveraged the best of the company's valuable and distinct resources while creating a view of a strong single company to the customers. To enable this, he enrolled executive management sponsors to support a program called Total Enterprise Account Management (TEAM).

The concept was based on a commitment to implement best practices in the development and maintenance of business with major customers. To complement his experience in growing a small private business, Charlie engaged CPS to help him design and execute his plan. With CPS, Charlie developed a strong and scalable customer-focused sales agenda. The TEAM concept was transformed into a prioritized yet flexible set of customer-focused initiatives with specific milestones and defined metrics.

Charlie and the CPS consulting team selected the following four most important initiatives of MSC's selling culture transformation.

Elevate the sales function. In a company whose focus for several years had been acquisitions, the most valued skills were associated with targeting and analyzing acquisition candidates, and integrating them while managing expenses and costs. Charlie recognized that the role of the salesperson was unclear and the value of the sales force was under-recognized. This prompted a reevaluation, redefinition, and elevation of selling team roles, responsibilities, and desired skill sets.

Develop a culture of responsibility and accountability. The executive management team gained an understanding of the critical importance of defining and documenting MSC's approach to account management. They applied recognized best practices in account management execution to MSC's desired future state of providing recognized customer value. The processes that emerged rounded out the TEAM concept and enabled management to define a four-step process for customer engagements with supporting tools that had both internal and external outcomes.

Establish a management discipline. To ensure consistent management review and consistent coaching, Charlie's team developed a documented management review process that identified leadership roles in active selling engagements, regular management reviews, and ongoing team coaching.

Develop a compensation and recognition system that drives results. To encourage sales personnel from different heritage organizations to work together, a compensation plan was developed that rewarded cross-business unit selling based on MSC's performance as well as the individual's performance.

The Outcome?

MSC continues to build a customer-driven company providing differentiated service to its clients. Everyone from the CEO to branch office personnel knows that things are different—there is a new energy, a new focus, and improving business results.

Charlie Davis offers the following advice to others who are undertaking a disciplined approach to providing recognizable value to customers.

- It all starts and ends with the customer.
- As a leader, you must be passionate about serving the customer.
- Be clear in everything you do.
- Instill a sense of urgency and compete to win.
- Recognize that a major part of the transformation is selling internally.
- Make decisions and stick with them.

Charlie admits that the battle for transformation is still being fought on a daily basis. "We still have different levels of enrollment," he says. "The effect of change directly hits the individual comfort zones of many of our employees." Reconciling new roles, sharing control, and sharing recognition with a team are all challenges that Charlie and the MSC leadership team are working diligently to address. As Charlie cautions, "This is not for the faint of heart."

Chapter Summary

Consistent attention to elements of good account management, as represented in the AME model, can have significant positive effects on major account success. The AME model works well to assess where the selling organization's abilities to fulfill the needs of its most important customers line up. The model helps a company look at complex processes required for strategic customer relationships and demystifies them into sustainable win-win, business-to-business relationships that, if nurtured, will yield extraordinary results. Moving forward with consistent targeted actions results in a tight cycle of value with key customers that bring continued and ever-greater rewards for both parties.

10

The Case for Relationship Investments

People buy from people they know and trust. If trust is there, they will create a rationale for doing business.
—*Mary Ann Costello, partner, Critical Path Strategies*

Academically, the chief sales officer agenda helps top sales executives identify major structural barriers to sustainable growth. In a similar vein, the account management execution model provides keen insight into critical gaps that must be addressed to consistently deliver customer value. And while a thorough and thoughtful approach is invaluable to establish an efficient and actionable selling organization strategy, we all know that nothing can be accomplished if we neglect the concept of people and relationship-building.

Over the years, we have heard chief sales officers and customers alike complain about the nature of the buyer/seller relationship. Customers express frustration that sales representatives simply do not listen to them, choosing instead to jump right into selling their product or service of the day. CSOs voice their own frustration about their representatives who call too low in the customer's organization, and do not think expansively about the importance of enrolling advocates at all levels.

In this chapter, we will review a few concepts that we have seen great sales leaders introduce to selling teams with significant results. The real key to success lies not in the individual concepts, but in the commitment a sales leader must make to help team members learn to identify, create, develop, and nurture intentional relationships.

Relationships with customers are the lifeblood of selling organizations. The question to ask is, "Do these relationships bring results for my selling organization, or are they only built around transactions that, when complete, do not create additional opportunity?"

Salespeople should work on developing different *kinds* of relationships at different *levels* in the customer organization hierarchy. This *fabric of relationships* should be woven across the customer organization so resiliently that it can withstand the uncertainties of both business life and human nature.

Salespeople intuitively know that they can advance their strategic goals by leveraging relationships at the business-to-business level to help close specific sales opportunities, and through personal relationships.

In general, most people like a *background of relatedness* for their business activities. They develop relationships internally and externally, but they need a context for the relationship. At its base is the answer to the question, "Why should I invest my time developing a relationship with this person?" This context or background of relatedness gives them a sense of stability. The perception of how a seller behaves, and what he does to help a customer, are the determinants of the value he brings.

When sales and customer teams jointly identify an extraordinary outcome for both parties, develop a plan to achieve it, and then execute the plan, they can develop long-lasting, high-value relationships. Ultimately, these relationships enable the customer and the selling organization to achieve their extraordinary goal and create the urgency to make it possible. In the following pages, we discuss some proven strategies and techniques for getting the most from customer relationships, and *getting the magic.* This is demonstrated by a passion for action by leadership in both customer and selling organizations.

Relationship-Development Strategy

Selling organizations need to ask themselves these questions.

- What is our strategy to discover customer business drivers?
- Who are the right people in the customer organization with whom we can align our mutual interests?
- Who are the people in our selling organization that should have responsibility for each key person in the customer organization?

- How do we take action and measure the selling organization's progress in actively building customer relationships?

Crucial throughout the sales process is the need to determine (and validate frequently) *who* will make the buying decision. World-class salespeople know that even the very best proposition may go unsold if the right customer players are not identified and thoughtful value propositions are not established with each player in the buying organization.

Organizational Mapping

The structure of most organization hierarchies has significantly changed during the last 20 years. Often referred to as flattening, matrixing, or leveling, this change has introduced new complexity for sales teams in determining *who* has authority, responsibility, and accountability for decisions.

This trend makes the classic organizational chart ineffective as a map or guide to who will make the ultimate decision. Frequently, the logic behind organizational flattening is to improve the speed of the decision cycle process and to drive new initiatives in highly competitive environments. Sales leaders who employ techniques that mirror this speed have a distinct advantage.

The most efficient salespeople stay abreast of organizational dynamics in this fast-paced environment. They employ techniques and tools to assure they know early, and accurately, who will make the decision, who will approve it, who will influence it, and who will implement the decision. By mapping and updating the client decision process, best-of-breed salespeople clarify client decision-making roles and assure focused selling time on the most important people.

Clients appreciate salespeople who can distill and react to their decision process, because it saves the client time and expense. Also, it adds to their confidence that the supplier/partner will perform efficiently once given the contract or commitment to move forward with the proposition. They begin to demonstrate trust.

The CPS Organizational-Mapping Technique

We work with clients to mine their best thinking on relationship strategy development. We encourage them to make organization charts come to life through mapping.

Picture a collaborative meeting. The sales leader illustrates on a diagram the following roles people will play in a buying process.

Decision maker. The person who directs the analysis and evaluation and makes the final decision on the project and suppliers to be employed.

Approver. The *economic buyer*. Typically, a senior executive from whom the decision maker gets final authority for a project or acquisition. Sometimes a steering or management committee performs this function. The approver normally has broad functional responsibility and decision-making authority, and often fiduciary responsibility.

Key user. Individuals in areas that directly benefit from the project and who articulate the *on-the-ground* business need.

Influencer (internal and external). People who could influence key executives, such as analysts, consultants, competitive sales personnel, professionals who might be charged with project management, contacts in other companies, and even relatives.

Change agent. Respected leader who has the courage and capacity to lead people and organizations in transformational change. Sometimes appointed. Sometimes self-appointed.

Gatekeeper. A person who decides who will be allowed entry into the competition. Often this person can say no to a vendor during the pre-bid vendor selection, but may not be involved in the final selection process. They manage access.

Analyst. Usually a staff person who assesses the technical or financial merits and feasibility of the proposal.

Before client names are placed in these roles, the team debates specifics, such as a person's role in this decision, accountability, authority, and influence. This technique inevitably leads to crystallization and consolidation of what is fact and what must be learned. A set of excellent questions, timed appropriately and directed at the heart of the sales process, is distilled from this exercise.

After the initial collaboration effort, the sales team can efficiently begin to validate or determine the reality of the client's decision process. The individuals identified in the mapping exercise are the clients who stand to benefit from this proposal. Therefore, a series of specific calls are planned as validation checkpoints and selling targets. These calls help determine key business initiatives and personal needs, and gain further insight into the decision-making process.

The map is further developed to pictorially draw needed lines of influence and optimal sales coverage. Individuals with a neutral or negative position toward the proposal are identified and highlighted. The map pinpoints these people for coverage with sales calls and positive sales information as part of a collaborative team effort. The team is able to create a thoughtful plan and avoid negative surprises as the selling campaign proceeds.

Without the mapping exercise, crucial sales strategies are often overlooked or are not communicated to the team. A consistent message can more easily be developed when all sales and support people see the same picture of the client. Mapping results in efficient use of sales time, and the client is spared potential confusion or redundant coverage. This is especially important when multiple salespeople call within a single client organization.

Organizational mapping also begs the question of what must be learned about the buying process. A set of key questions is developed using assumptions to validate or determine the reality of a client's decision process. The quality of the questions is critical because they require answers (calls on key clients) that feed the development of sound, client-centric sales strategies and gain competitive advantage for the selling firm.

The sales team gains crucial insight by developing and sharing the map with all members of the team and, in some cases, even the client. In an example of one client campaign in which CPS was engaged, the selling team identified a client change agent who, when asked, validated and shared specific insight into a unique decision process. This knowledge saved extensive time and energy for both firms. By sharing the map with the client change agent, the team was able to quickly correct a situation and win a very successful sales campaign. Some of our clients call these people their champion.

Organizational mapping assures that the sales effort optimizes valuable time and validates appropriate client coverage. An additional advantage is the improved efficiency this tool brings to pre-call briefings. New team members, or people outside the team who are brought into the sales effort, quickly understand client dynamics and can better react in a call or presentation. Using this technique for sales planning, and keeping it current with knowledge gained during client calls, will increase the odds of closing sales and allow clients to see the sales team as a highly valued partner.

Zippering

Another key concept additive to organizational mapping is one of aligning relationships—*zippering*. Zippered relationships establish accountability for key relationships and orchestrate interactions at many corresponding levels in both the selling and customer organizations. Specific selling team members are aligned with their counterparts in the customer organization. For example, accounts receivable in the seller's organization interacts with accounts payable in the customer's. Here are examples of more matching roles.

Seller/Buyer Roles Alignment

Selling Organization	Customer Company
General counsel	General counsel
Administrative officer	Purchasing officer
Research and development scientist	Engineers
Technical support officer	Application developer
Sales representative	User department executive
Technology account executive	Chief information officer
Chief financial officer	Chief financial officer
President	President

To the extent that sellers can identify contact points like these and enroll them onto the selling team, they can protect themselves against the inevitable pulls and strains on that primary decision maker. It is also a way to uncover greater value, since any of these contacts may point them to an opportunity, or may have some influence that they may not have known.

The salesperson now can use his expanded selling team to bridge and communicate with the customer organization. The salesperson's own outside perspective can be very valuable to the customer, of course, but it can also surface information, insights, and opportunities for the seller.

"Show Me the Value-Added Benefits!"

Remember the movie, *Jerry Maguire*, in which the aspiring National Football League player shouts at his agent, "Show me the money!" What customers are shouting is, "Show me what else you can do for me!" We were recently engaged by a client to interview 10 of their most important customers. One of the questions we asked was, "What else could this logistics firm do for you and your business?" The response was immediate and clear: *the four Cs*.

1. Bring me more *creative* ideas

2. *Challenge* me

3. Help me *change*

4. Help me stay in *control*

There is another powerful variation. Show me the money has become: *Show me the money and other value-added benefits.* The value the customer wants is just about anything he perceives to be valuable to him, to his company, and to the company's future. That could be financial gain, best-practices benchmarking, enhancement of reputation, competitive advantage, technology sharing, reliability, innovation, empathy, and a range of other benefits. This kind of extra-value-based relationship is not a luxury. It is what customers increasingly expect from sellers.

We have interviewed hundreds of our clients' customers. They have high expectations of prospective partners. From the customer's point of view, value could encompass any or all of the following needs.

Understand me

- Be a world-class listener, listen every day; things change
- If you are part of the process, you will be part of the solution
- Be there

Be my focal point

- To the outside world
- To others in my organization

Understand my alternatives

- Understand my responsibilities to senior management and to others in my organization
- Understand my constraints (do not take it personally)

Make me a winner

- Make everyone on my team a winner
- Become the most important person on my team

Sellers need to focus on their customers' most important personal and professional issues. That means working on relationships in some way every day. What are the key relationship initiatives that our team is focused on for a particular customer, and how do they affect the customer's current priorities? The seller's relationship actions are driven by what the customer is trying to do and what the selling organization wants to achieve with this customer. The actions develop from a common focus on what the seller and customer can do together to get to a desired state. Whatever type of product or service, sellers provide specific relationship initiatives that could help address many customer issues.

- Fix quality problems
- Focus on safety
- Provide joint marketing activities
- Encourage joint research and development or new technology collaboration
- Enable executive-to-executive planning

Sellers should enlarge these relationships in ways that are appropriate to the customer's interests, because the deepening relationships will give them greater insight into how to serve those interests in more and better ways. The better ways involve what we call value deliverables, or *gifts.*

Gifts Beget Gifts

Consistently successful salespeople make a practice of consistently providing extra value or services, or gifts, to the customer in the context of their relationship. These gifts are the favors sellers do, insights they provide, and assistance they give to the customer outside of, or tangential to, their business with that customer. They are gifts that solidify the relationship. Like gifts given on special occasions, they are meaningful to the participant and nothing is expected in return.

By packaging and presenting gifts appropriately, sellers are doing something beneficial for a customer needing personal or professional help and guidance. They are taking major actions outside the conversation of selling. We call these *high-value actions.* These actions enable a seller to become a trusted advisor, someone who can act as a consultant for the customer and collaborate with him on ways to succeed. Here are some examples of high-value actions.

- Solve something small incredibly well
- Facilitate a planning session
- Be a recruiting resource
- Introduce business prospects
- Provide referrals
- Bring trade information on topics of interest to customer
- Offer analysis and problem-solving
- Offer perspectives and recommendations
- Mentor customer's staff

- Invite customer to present to your peers at conferences
- Provide competitive analysis
- Ask customer to review draft presentation and vice versa
- Provide access to insights from your research and development
- Help with problems unrelated to your business
- Offer insights about what your other best clients are doing

Going the extra mile, providing special help, and giving the client a new perspective on an issue—all these things might be considered extraneous to the job of selling. They are, in fact, *fundamental* to the job of creating customer acceptance of salespeople and the company they represent.

When a seller acts as friend, coach, consultant, counselor, advisor, even partner to the customer, the customer begins to see the seller and the seller's company differently. The customer will not find it difficult to make the step to seeing the seller's offering differently. Over time, the fact that the salesperson is a vendor will even start to recede in his mind.

These gifts enable selling organizations to be there when extraordinary opportunities present themselves, and to earn the right to be given special consideration. That is a gift from the buyer to the seller. The buyer, in turn, gains a stable relationship from a supplier that can meet his needs—with less work. Loyalty does pay—all around. It is a self-sustaining cycle of value for the seller and the customer.

Cover Me Correctly

One of our client's biggest concerns is how his suppliers' selling teams work with him and his team. He knows that some of his suppliers have great talents that could help him to achieve a competitive edge. But how can he discover these? How effectively do those suppliers *cover* him? As he puts it, "How do I get them to show me what they have?" This is particularly difficult for customers when most suppliers are focused on short-term and tactical issues. This phenomenon makes suppliers who invest in customer-centered relationship activities extremely valuable to customers, and positions the supplier for significant business opportunities. The problem for this senior executive is that he must depend on the suppliers to make the decision to invest in his success, in the right way.

Obviously, busy salespeople cannot afford to invest the time or energy to develop high-value relationships with every account nor everyone in any account. There just is not the time or energy to stretch their resources that far.

They need to deploy resources for developing relationships for those customers who will most likely *respond the best* to what they are offering. The organizational mapping exercise helps identify who those people might be.

There is a simple axiom for this concept. *Relationship-building does not pay off everywhere; sellers need to be selective.* The seller needs to be discriminating about which relationships will be the most beneficial. Sellers need to assign relationship resources to accounts selectively—not democratically. For example, a customer whose primary business strategy is to buy at the lowest price may not be particularly interested in added value. Also, the corporate culture of some companies makes them poor candidates for relationship-building. If they do not treat their own people or their customers well, they are not likely to treat a supplier well either.

A customer that is focused on areas like total cost of operation, revenue growth, or risk mitigation, however, is a good candidate for a seller's relationship-building efforts. Change agents in customer organizations who lead projects that sellers can influence are the best candidates for a proactive relationship-building investment.

Clients will respond openly to the *right kind* of relationship actions by sellers. This does not necessarily involve more people, or higher caliber people on the account, but sometimes just different capabilities and actions. The operative customer phrase here is, *cover me correctly.* Sellers need to find the type of resource that the customer would value the most, and then apply that resource to the relationship.

Second, when sellers are selective about how they relate to a particular customer, it is a determining factor in how buyers perceive the seller's offering. Buyers do not want sellers to waste resources on relationships that do not warrant the attention.

> When CPS partner, Ken Evans, headed the 1,100-person sales force for a $10-billion environmental management services company, he discovered that the executive of a potential customer abhorred the administrative costs of managing the billing for waste and recycling service across thousands of locations.
>
> People calling on this executive in the past were busy driving transactions, not listening to the root issue. Ken's firm invested in systems that consolidated billing and other administrative tasks, which he could then offer to address the customer's needs. It worked and he was able to grow revenue from this customer from $2 million to $16 million in a year.

"You have to listen really well," says Ken. "We applied strategic resources to a strategic problem." How did the customer view Ken's company? "We became the role model for the services part of their business," he says. "They asked us to work with their other suppliers to put a similar model in place. Neither party focused on price, but both achieved greater profits, and this billing investment was replicable for 90 other of the firm's most important customers. Customer-driven equals market-driven."

If sellers do not indicate that they are sensitive to customers' requirements (for example, providing full service coverage for an account that just needs maintenance), customers may lose confidence in the seller and even be irritated. They think, "If this supplier cannot figure out how to use his own resources well, how will he serve my interests? Will he waste my resources, too?"

One of the greatest challenges for sales leaders, therefore, is to balance the timing and intensity of selling efforts relative to the circumstances at hand, and take the most appropriate actions to yield the best results. They need to put the right amount of pressure on each element of each sales opportunity and relationship initiative. They cannot spend the same amount of time on all of them, all the time.

If a seller focuses on two to four customer relationships to cultivate for truly high value, the results will likely be one to three new *permanent friends* a year. Typically, the seller never finishes developing the account relationship. Priorities change, people move, other urgent issues get in the way. The rewards, however, can be truly incredible.

Tighter Relationships: Two Scenarios

As the value of the relationship and the value of the seller's offerings to a customer become more intertwined, possibilities open up for an even greater exchange of value for both parties. The prize, or payoff—for seller and customer—is an even higher level of collaboration yielding higher levels of success for both. The customer can justify buying the seller's offering at a higher price than competitors because of the additional, quantifiable value that the seller brings to that customer. The selling organization has built a bank of institutional knowledge and invested in relationships as well as intellectual capital.

Greater Value All Around

How would a loyal customer of your organization respond to criticism for not taking a cheaper alternative? These are the types of responses we hope for.

- The way they put their solution together to fit our needs is what sets them apart. Their solution will help us substantially improve our availability and reduce our risk.

- This supplier will help us implement the key business initiative six months early, which more than covers the full cost of their products and services.

- Because of significant contributions they have made in the past, they have become a key part of our leadership team.

- We cannot afford to lose them, nor for them to not be profitable. They are critical to our future.

Loyal customers will call such a seller when they have a need; they will buy at a fair price, even if it is higher than alternatives. They will speak highly of you and your company because you represent significant, quantifiable value. Customers save resources and exponentially expand their team's talent pool by getting what they need from selected high-value suppliers.

So, if this really is what the seller wants the customer to say, what actions will cause the customer to justify a commitment to the seller? Many salespeople are now familiar with examples of seller-customer collaboration that brought greater value to both. This practice is becoming more commonplace, as buyers try to maximize the value they get from suppliers in an increasingly fast-paced and commoditized market, and sellers try to focus their efforts on the best returns for the energy invested in customer relationships.

Siemens is a major customer of Marriott. The account representative for Marriott discovered that Siemens had a business need to develop a presence in Eastern Europe and grow its business there. However, their executives could not find appropriate accommodations there while they undertook that work.

So, Marriott and Siemens formed a business partnership. Siemens acquired property, and Marriott built hotels on that property. As the partnership continued, trade-offs brought them both advantages. Siemens enjoyed price breaks on hotel stays, and Marriott was able to use Siemens technology in its construction activities.

This high-value collaborative undertaking was not just luck. The salesperson did not just happen to talk to a particular executive about this issue by chance one day. There was already a high-value relationship established between the two companies.

The selling organization had cultivated and deepened this relationship over time. They had established a high level of trust and value delivery. They had zippered the two organizations as closely as was appropriate. They had done their homework, and earned the right to be the right choice.

The Dark Side

The future also has a darker side for which selling organizations need to be prepared. Even fruitful relationships will have inevitable pressures and strains placed on them, as a natural part of the thrust and parry of business dynamics. Sellers are at risk at every moment.

It would be gratifying if all the work they put into developing high-value customer relationships would continue to flow benefits to them and their customers. Count on this instead: *Something will happen to change things.*

Here is a scenario. You are in a high-value relationship with a key person in the customer organization. There is new pressure in that organization to reduce costs in the area that you supply. Your customer contact is pressured to reevaluate your arrangement. What benefits can you demonstrate for him not to go to bid?

- Itemize the many other value-added benefits the customer enjoys from the arrangement
- Cite the fair price, and low total cost of ownership of your solution
- Ask how long it would likely take for another supplier to get up to speed to even approximate the value you are now delivering

Do you have this level of relationship with a customer? It is your only defense in a cutthroat environment. In one way or another, suppliers are going to get squeezed. They will encounter aggressive budget squeezes; they will see new competitors ready to pounce on their turf, they will see ruthless players try to ambush your relationships for political ends. The business environment is in continual flux and the pace is quickening.

There is broader economic reason for selling organizations to hold on tight to good customers. The ebbs and flows of national and global economic cycles profoundly affect all businesses. Because these ups and downs are much less predictable in timing, direction, and duration, selling organizations must be able to survive the downswings profitably, and prepare to take advantage of the upswings early. Investing in customer relationships and consistently articulating and delivering value is the only secure way to accomplish that. This balance of the buyer-seller relationship is the only truly sustainable operating model for successful selling organizations.

Chapter Summary

The real key to success in a selling organization is to create and invest in long-lasting, high-value relationships with customers. Organizational mapping is an excellent tool to validate appropriate client coverage and explore possible relationship strategies, specifically relative to identifying the decision maker in a customer's buying process.

Customers look to their suppliers as a value resource. Sales teams need to be diligent in providing market intelligence, best practices, new technology, staff recommendations, and other valued *gifts* to customers to build value-based, collaborative relationships.

With organizations seemingly in constant flux, sometimes, for reasons beyond a salesperson's control, something will change to threaten the high-value relationship with a customer. It is important that salespeople prepare and be alert for these changes. Remember the mantra: *Act like you are about to lose the customer to the competition—before it becomes a reality.*

11

Leverage Relationship Investments

If you have a strong base of relationships, you can get a lot more results with a lot less energy.

—Gene Batchelder, chief information officer and senior vice president of administration, ConocoPhillips

Everyone knows that good customer relationships are necessary to identify and drive big opportunities for sellers and buyers. Relationships provide the conduit for everything sellers need for success—information, new ideas, warning signs, verification, new opportunities, and revenue. To be prepared for extraordinary results, relationship development must be undertaken intentionally.

The big question for salespeople is, "Why should I invest time and resources in relationships beyond the immediate sale?" Many would add, "I cannot stretch my time and energy that far. We are getting bashed every day on price, and I have huge quarterly earnings targets. We will have to put that investment off." Sadly, that time never comes. The next quarter arrives and everyone in the selling organization is focused only on relationships around current opportunities, which seldom pay off in long-term, high-value relationships.

How do sellers know whether their offering carries the most value for this customer; that the influencers are really in their court? They need to invest considerable time and effort—off the top of their already busy schedule—in developing relationships that will give them that knowledge and more.

- If sellers do not carve out time for these kinds of actions, they will have to work harder later to keep this customer, and even harder to get new ones.

- In the medium-to-long-term, it takes less time to treat customers the right way than to rush around reacting to short-term priorities—but few sales leaders act this way!

Good customer relationships help customers more easily get answers to the questions, "Why buy anything?" and "Why buy from this seller?" Relationships also enable sellers to develop the business case for, "Why buy now?" Our experience and research tell us that most salespeople spend precious little time in front of their customers. In this chapter, we explore the implications, both good and bad, of how selling organization time is used.

Investments of Time

Unfortunately, for customers and their suppliers, the investment in building good buyer-seller relationships is becoming increasingly opportunistic. Investments of time in relationship-building tend to focus on short-term, active sales situations and issues caused by the lack of a pro-active relationship focus. People pay attention to short-term deals, and attend to short-term priorities. The relationships from these near-sighted encounters do not produce the kinds of deep and fruitful relationships that sustain sellers and their companies.

This trend in the selling environment creates a tremendous opportunity for those sales leaders who force their selling teams to intentionally invest in the right relationships at the right time and in the right way in anticipation of opportunity. Smart sellers develop and execute *proactive and deliberate strategies for building relationships* that lead to profitable results.

In a cutthroat competitive environment, many buyers fixate on price, and sellers accommodate them by focusing their relationship time around current sales opportunities late in the buying cycle. Sellers who do that run the risk of losing to a lower-cost supplier, or winning a deal that is unprofitable. Chasing small sales opportunities to the detriment of building important relationships will not get salespeople far on the way to their goals, much less extraordinary performance.

Successful selling organizations intentionally focus on customer outcomes and key people in key accounts as part of a targeted sales strategy. Many organizations make a big production of account team planning for their sales future. They identify compelling value solutions for targeted customers. They generate great ideas in brainstorming sessions. They get revved up for performance. Then, not much really happens. Why? Cultural inertia is one reason, as we discussed. Many salespeople naturally spend most of their time with people they know and like, versus investing time with people who can influence the extraordinary sale.

A client of ours made a big investment in an account team planning session for a newly restructured sales organization. They identified their largest opportunities for growth, and put some of their best people on the key accounts. They identified solid value solutions. They had great ideas in their planning sessions, significant opportunity was identified, and team members solemnly committed to invest in relationships.

Several months later, a follow-up session was held for the sales leadership, including account and solutions leaders. Almost nothing had happened since the initial planning sessions. Senior sales team members had committed to identify key people in target customers' lines of businesses; they had not done so. They had been expected to conduct a gap assessment to see if their original value proposition was still relevant with a particular customer, but they had not done so.

In one major account, when the reviewing sales executive challenged the lack of relationship execution, they all discovered that a low-level customer contact had told the company's salespeople that the company was a valued and important supplier. The salespeople were almost at the point of forecasting a long-term multimillion-dollar deal with this customer. On this basis they thought, "Why should we invest in other relationships?" A short time later, the customer's purchasing agent said to them, "Guys, I do not know how to tell you this, but we just gave a two-year, sole-sourced order to one of your biggest competitors."

What happened? The sales team knew they had responsibility for developing relationships. They had committed to, but not held themselves accountable for, short-term actions directed to cultivating those relationships. They became complacent. They believed what the low-level customer contact told them, and did not pursue other relationships further—the relationships their competitor had cultivated.

This loss was a big wake-up call for the selling organization. Fortunately, there were still other significant opportunities with this customer. The executive sponsor for the account made calls on high-level people in the customer organization and sponsored new proposals. Within a few months, the company had secured a new, sizeable contract with this customer, and because of the relationships built, eventually earned the right to win over the competitor who had superseded them.

Consider the contacts that salespeople call on in their key accounts. It is human nature to talk to people we like and who like us, people with whom we feel comfortable. In an exercise we conduct with sales groups, we ask participants to identify three people in the customer organization for whom they would take ownership of the relationship. Invariably, they name people with whom they are familiar or comfortable. They like making *milk-and-cookie calls* on these people. They are always welcome. They always have a good conversation, but often do not move the ball forward.

Salespeople are likely to avoid calling on customers they perceive to be negative toward their company. That perception could be the result of a bad experience, poor personal chemistry, or the hard-nosed reputation of a customer contact or executive. Usually, these are indeed perceptions which focused actions can overcome.

When we compare the participants' choices to an organizational map of the client organization, we often discover the apparently negative contacts are important decision makers or influencers in the customer organization, critical to shaping the value the seller could provide. Our advice is always to first focus on the apparently negative contacts in addition to their circle of influence, to round out their organizational buying process picture. There is another reason for hesitancy: not knowing the value of sales calls to the selling organization's big picture.

What Is a Good Investment of Time?

Sellers have an obligation to know their customer's business well enough to provide a valuable offering, and a responsibility to cultivate a high-value relationship with them that confers benefits on their organization as well. We will start with trying to quantify the value of customer calls for the eventual value they could bring.

What if a salesperson believed that the average value of every customer call was $150,000? How important would they treat those calls? Would they spend their relationship time in the same way, with the same people, as they do now? Consider the following scenario.

Costs

- Goal of four high-impact meetings or sales calls per week, or 200 per year
- Compensation plus sales overhead of $300,000 per person
- Cost of each sales call: $1,500 per call

Value to Our Company

- Assume the sales representative's revenue goal is 10 times his "all-in cost," or $3 million
- 200 calls to achieve the goal brings the value to $15,000 per meeting

Value to the Customer

- Assume the customer expects 10 times the value in return for the $3 million they invest
- The 200 calls that help the customer realize $30 million of value translates to $150,000 per meeting

This investment of high-quality calls is overwhelming in its return to the salesperson, the selling company, and the customer.

The message: *Increase the number of sales calls focused on the right people, and be prepared for highly effective calls and meetings.*

Getting a Customer's Share of Mind and Time

How many account managers do you think are trying to sell to Fortune 500 companies? SAMA estimates this number to be 500,000 in the United States alone. Every sales representative is expected to get access to, call on, and develop relationships with some of the senior management in these companies. That means that half a million salespeople are trying to reach a few thousand senior executives in these Fortune 500 companies. Obviously, only a few will succeed.

How does a sales professional break in? How do sales leaders set an example for developing great relationships that lead to great results, and guide salespeople in this important activity?

We might think a compelling value proposition for the seller's offering, endorsed by an important influencer or decision maker, is the ticket to customers' time and share of mind. When a buyer decides to invest in a relationship with a seller, however, a big factor in their decision is having positive answers to the questions, "What is in it for my organization?" and "What is in it for me?" In many cases, what is in it for them goes beyond the immediate proposal. The value of the relationship often becomes part of the business value of the offering. The value proposition of the *relationship* promotes the customer's rationale and buy-in for the value proposition of the *offering*.

The value of the relationship is not something that is cultivated off-site to advance the business connections around business interests. Too many salespeople believe that a dinner or golf outing will get it done. But buyers are busy.

Dinner or golf with a stranger and without clear business value is the last thing they are looking to do. One of our clients put this succinctly, "I always have people wanting to take me on social events to build the relationship. I think, show me the value first, and then I will get to know you better. Right now, I prefer to have dinner with my family!"

Good relationships with executives are built piece-by-piece, call-by-call, and experience-by-experience with a range of customer contacts. They are based on value for the customer at every point of contact. In the next sections, we will explore successively more rewarding ways of getting to the value for the customer, and how to go higher and tighter in important customer relationships.

Testing Assumptions

Customers, of course, know quite a lot about sellers. They know more about sellers and competitors today than at any point in time. They have accumulated enormous amounts of information from the Internet and other sources to analyze the suppliers of goods and services. Sellers need to balance this wholesale knowledge about them and their rivals with precise knowledge of their customers and the individuals within them.

The selling organization must frame the underlying value of all it can offer to a customer and deliver the value message across the customer's organization. In short, it needs to get *crisp* on the net value it can provide to the customer and align that message to each individual.

In their zeal to *run the play faster*, many sales leaders and salespeople charge toward what they think is the finish line on the basis of skewed or false assumptions, and end up with only wasted effort. They could have worked smarter if they had validated their information in advance. Every conversation with the customer, at every level, with every sales representative, helps to reduce the risk of false assumptions about what the customer wants or needs.

> In one client engagement, we held a one-day relationship workshop with an experienced account team to determine how well aligned the selling organization's perception of customer needs was with the customer's actual needs. The team had been unsuccessful to date and was frustrated.
>
> We asked account team members to record what they thought were this particular customer's most important initiatives and values. We asked the group to rank these in order of importance. Then we invited the selected customer to join us. The customer shared his most impor-

tant initiatives and his suggestions for how the seller could help the most. The team subsequently recorded the executive's comments.

We compared the two versions. There was a substantial gap. The account team had been working on a set of assumptions that were apparently never tested with the customer. This meant that most of their conversations had been wasteful for both them and the client.

Following the meeting, the team leader called in the customer to thank him. The customer was impressed with the number and quality of people in the meeting, and appreciated the team investing time to better understand his business. He gave them direction in several areas that could lead to better relationships and results the following year.

The team was humbled, but also excited about the new-found opportunities. They significantly changed the way they listened to and serviced that client. The selling organization had made time to discover what the customer's key objectives/initiatives were, and created solutions to support those initiatives. Now they were on the right track. They had information, confidence, and the beginnings of a strategy.

As a result of this experience, our client sponsored an additional 40, one-day relationship sessions with individual customers in the next two months and doubled the company's active pipeline of sales opportunities. The result? This helped the sales executive and his team grew their business tenfold in five years.

Even an experienced team can miss the heart of the issues around which they are working, despite the best of intentions and using accepted strategies and techniques. Sales teams need to know the customer's business drivers at the corporate level and for each line of business that they can touch. They need to look at all the things they can provide to that customer. They need to find the highest value linkages between their company and that customer. If they do these things well, they will demonstrate customer intimacy and willingness to partner. Trust, and business, will result.

At CPS, we help clients identify those things for which the customer would change his buying habits, and develop strategies and action plans for successful outcomes. We encourage clients to discover and understand, through active listening, the customer's needs or aspirations, and the most important ways they can help that customer. Sales teams with this knowledge can do more right things earlier with the customer, which develop and deepen the relationship, preparing them to achieve extraordinary results.

Customer Conversations: Getting Crisper

Conversations with the customer are at the heart of all sales activities. Relationships provide the basis for the value that both buyer and seller discover. The quality of conversations is what moves relationships forward. These high-value conversations occur from prospecting, throughout the sales process, to closure, when the secured solution is handed off to the delivery team.

One of the greatest gifts you can provide to a customer is to clarify the customer's value proposition to *his* customer. This involves articulating how his customer validates value, how it is measured, and how it is recognized by *his* customer. The value to you is tremendous.

It might start like this. Say you have an opportunity to speak with a senior executive of the customer organization. Here is a series of questions that can get you both to the beginning of what could be a high-value relationship.

- Before we start talking about our offerings, can we take a few minutes to step back and talk about your organization?

- Can you describe how your customers view your organization when you are at your best?

Most people will begin by speaking in positive terms, about the high value they provide, how long they have retained certain customers, perhaps some testimonials. You might then draw out some not so idyllic features.

- What are the biggest difficulties that could keep you from continuing to achieve success with your customers?

- If you are successful in overcoming these issues, what kinds of results would your customers see?

- What two or three key initiatives do you think would help you achieve your primary objectives with your customers?

- For these initiatives, what are your goals for next year?

- Who would be involved in getting these accomplished? How would progress be measured?

- What are the key things that you expect to be doing in the next few months to support this vision?

- We have successful experience with some of our customers in working similar initiatives—which one of these areas would you like to explore first?

By engaging in these conversations, you are on the road to developing your own value proposition for this customer by talking about his value proposition to his customer. Here again, you are demonstrating an orientation to the client's business issues and then, and only then, introducing how you might align with them. This conversation theme about his customer almost always creates a sense of excitement and urgency.

In this way, you recognize—always with greater clarity—what the customer values; and the customer recognizes the many dimensions of value that you might provide to his organization.

Your Value in the Customer's Words

The next step up from customers recognizing and acknowledging the seller's value is for customers to be willing to speak about that value to others in their organization. That is a powerful marketing tool for the selling organization. However, it comes only when real, recognizable value has been demonstrated and delivered by the seller.

> One of the best testaments to a selling organization's effectiveness with key customers is for them to tell their peers about how good the seller is. One of our colleagues asked a CEO, "Why do you keep doing business with that supplier? There are lots of others who are just as good who would like your business, and I am sure there are some that are significantly lower in price."
>
> The CEO replied, "Because they act every day like they are about to lose our business to the competition."
>
> Our colleague persisted. "What do you mean by that? What does your supplier do to win that kind of loyalty from you?" "Well," said the CEO, "this supplier is professional, enthusiastic, and well organized, responds quickly when required, and always tries to understand my business." The CEO gave the following summary of value demonstrated by this supplier.
>
> - Calls on me, my internal constituents, and sometimes my customers regularly
>
> - Asks for input from me and other lines of business before presenting a proposal
>
> - Puts new solutions in front of me, without my asking, sometimes packaging things in different ways that suit my needs
>
> - Works effectively with all levels of my organization, respects our people and what they are trying to do

- Comes back after implementing a solution to see if we are happy with it and what benefits we have realized

- Communicates the value that I receive from their products and services

- Handles unforeseen problems with a sense of urgency and accountability

- Always exceeds their commitment

Actions like these can occur at all levels of both the customer's and seller's organizations. They are the seller's most potent actions toward becoming a trusted advisor. Trusted advisors can always get access and share of mind and time. The big opportunities and the big payoffs are at the level of high-value buyers.

The Customer: Know the Value before I Know It

Buyers continue to consolidate suppliers, squeeze costs, and demand high value for every nickel they spend. High-value buyers, however, present fantastic opportunities for high-value suppliers.

George Bishop, a long-time client, is the senior vice president of administration of a Fortune 50 corporation. There are 3,000 employees reporting to him, and thousands of suppliers that sell to his company. How can he discover what kind of value each of those suppliers can offer? This is a challenge for both George and the suppliers. "Give me a huge value proposition," says George, and he expects those who want his business to do just that.

It is the suppliers' obligation to know George's business well enough to convince him to have a relationship with their company. George admits, however, that he does not have time to know each of the suppliers and to understand each value proposition. This leaves him in a position where he needs to discover the right information about a select number of suppliers that can bring him extraordinary value.

George uses many of the principles we have been discussing to promote information technology in his own company. He has two account managers who develop business-to-business, personal, and solution relationships with end users. These relationships provide content about value opportunities: Who is doing what? Where is the edge? From that information, the information technology organization identifies the most important initiatives of their internal customers. That information, in turn, provides valuable information.

- Identifies the most critical initiatives that information technology needs to focus on

- Identifies suppliers that could positively impact the key initiatives

- Evaluates suppliers and their ability to execute against the key initiatives, and the potential reward for information technology from succeeding in the initiatives

The last criterion is a critical one. George expects potential suppliers to ensure that they have world-class account managers assigned to his account. He wants a supplier's best salespeople working on his most important initiatives. He wants them to understand and use their organization's best practices on his priorities.

There is more. George wants suppliers to have intimate knowledge of their organization's research and development activities and directions, and to have broad knowledge of their company's overall capabilities—in order to serve his interests. George says, "I want my partner (selected supplier) to know the value opportunity before I know. They win by knowing what I need, so I do not see them as just another supplier."

He is willing to treat some suppliers like customers—if those suppliers offer and deliver the best value to him. What he wants is for suppliers to help him accomplish his business objectives and create value for both of them. For sharp sellers, this is an incredible opportunity.

Sales leaders may be eager to steer their sales teams toward the exciting opportunities represented by customers like George, but this takes some homework.

Making Time for Internal Relationships

A substantial challenge for sales leadership is *selling* internal, non-salespeople effectively on selling organization objectives. Sales leaders need share of mind from their colleagues to get their commitment and participation so that which is sold is delivered with excellence. Salespeople also want them to have much the same enthusiasm for securing a piece of business as they do.

If non-salespeople do not clearly understand what they are expected to do, or why, to advance a particular opportunity, they will base their actions on their own experience and priorities. Those actions may not be what salespeople need them to do. Everyone—the selling organization members and non-sales colleagues in the company—should be taking the best next actions in a coordinated way to achieve extraordinary sales.

For each opportunity, engagement, and relationship, sales leaders must develop selective support and buy-in from various parts of the organization—finance, information technology, marketing, human resources, manufacturing, customer service, and others that may be appropriate. These people also need a solid understanding of the value proposition for each customer, and what sales is planning to do to move forward in each case.

If sellers can persuade their peers that cooperating with the selling organization on key sales initiatives is in the peers' own best interests, sellers can gain a valuable coalition of stakeholders to advance their goals. As we saw earlier, it is important for the selling organization to have the support of non-sales colleagues for the sales agenda and the priority items identified by the selling organization.

Best-of-the-best sales leaders treat everyone in their company in much the same manner as they treat customers, because selling internally is as important as selling externally.

Making the Case Internally for the Customer

The sales organization should be the customer's advocate within the seller's own organization. This can put sales leaders in an awkward position with some of the people with whom they work. In many cases, sales leaders will be a thorn in their non-sales colleagues' sides.

At times, it may be necessary for sellers to surface internal problems, and deliver the uncomfortable message *that their baby is ugly*. Customer problems and issues could include unresponsive customer service, products shipped late or with defects, billing issues, or competitive leadership.

A sales leader needs to make his associate aware of a situation in the associate's area of responsibility that could impact sales—and the whole company. He can then present the situation on a holistic business level, and suggest, "Here's what we need to do together to address this issue." He can add, "Here is what will happen if we do not."

He might pull out the income statement and invite his associate to consider what would happen if sales levels stay flat, as well as what could happen if sales improve by just 10 percent. He then might discuss the implications of each for the company. It is important to talk to associates in terms they can *hear and understand*. Any sales executive who cannot do that is at a disadvantage.

Whatever is necessary to help colleagues understand the selling organization's objectives and needs, and appreciate how they could contribute, should be done as energetically and as diplomatically as possible. The biggest challenge for sales leaders is to win over the organization so that the whole company considers itself part of the selling team.

Chapter Summary

Developing good professional relationships with customers is one of the best investments of time for sales leaders and their teams. Channeling relationship development into progressive actions that result in sales is the next challenge.

Developing relationships takes a conscious dedication of time and proactive and deliberate strategies. Every customer interaction is a moment of truth, an opportunity to further the relationship, so planning and orchestrating these encounters is a must.

To ensure that customers perceive value and benefit from each interaction, it is imperative that conversations with customers are oriented toward their business issues and how the sales team can align with them to help deliver on the customers' value propositions. Helping customers create value for their customers is magic.

PART 4.
INSTILL SALES LEADERSHIP RHYTHM AND COACHING

CHAPTER 12.
INSTILL SALES LEADERSHIP RHYTHM
CHAPTER 13.
CREATE SELLING ORGANIZATION ACCOUNTABILITY
CHAPTER 14.
COACH AND COMPENSATE SALES TEAMS FOR RESULTS

In previous chapters, we discussed ways for sales leaders to determine what the most important issues are for the company and the sales organization. We discussed the need for the sales organization to lead the company to execute its strategy, and how the real test of a company's strategy is its ability to execute in the marketplace, customer by customer. The chief sales officer must decide on an agenda, enroll the stakeholders, and get others to execute like their life depends on it.

In Part 2, we discussed how to make sure the selling organization's coverage model matches that strategy and, most importantly, aligns with customer expectations. This, in itself, requires leadership guts to make changes to the tried and true ways of the past, including reengineering internal processes to build a foundation for results.

In Part 3, we talked about execution. Solid plans, executed well, are far superior to elegant plans without the muscle to yield results. We explored some best practices of account management execution, and the importance of relationship management.

In Part 4, we will discuss some best practices of sales leadership, and the rhythm and discipline required to accomplish this. First, we will talk about the need for predictable leadership and the different roles leaders must play to *fly in formation*. Next, we will talk about implementing a review process that ensures accountability, and finally, coaching and compensating sales professionals to success.

12

Instill Sales Leadership Rhythm

We want wild ducks, but we need them to fly in formation.
—Tom Watson, Sr.

Think about how many of your sales colleagues over the years have had a series of increasingly more responsible jobs at major companies or new ventures. Why did some of these promising people succeed? Why did many of them fail?

Most sales leaders have had extensive selling experience. Often, a top executive started out as a rookie sales representative with an average territory. They managed to redefine the playing field and turn customer opportunities into winning transactions. At some point, their efforts were rewarded with a promotion to a first-line sales manager.

In this role, the new sales manager might have whipped the team into shape with sales heroics techniques acquired from the school of hard knocks, and squeezed out results with a great deal of personal blood, sweat, and tears. This performance led to another promotion to the next level of sales management, a tougher job. In that role, the leader was still deeply and personally involved in working with the team to help strategize on key opportunities and to help close deals.

We have seen something interesting in watching many bright young sales leaders progress in this manner. At some point, their span of control and their ability to personally impact a deal outruns their bandwidth. It is then that the sales manager and, by extension, the whole selling organization, begins to suffer. We can no longer afford the calendar time for every sales manager to experience this curve.

How do sales executives create a culture of personal accountability and solid execution within their selling teams? Great sales executives know that to do this they must translate their personal skills and best practices they have observed into a repeatable discipline for those they lead. They create and activate a process within the sales organization that is not dependent solely on their sales heroics, but rather on repeatable, predictable, outcome-based activities that can produce extraordinary results for their company.

Why the Selling Organization Needs Leadership Discipline

In every company, people who sell, deliver, and develop relationships with customers are its most important assets. They are the conduits to the company's ultimate asset: the customer. The sales leadership team is the organizational *owner* of this collective asset, and is obligated to manage and nurture it in a way that produces the best sustainable results.

That is a big obligation! The discipline of the leadership team promotes the sales agenda for every opportunity and engagement. By discipline we mean the commitment, persistence, and energy of sales leaders to cultivate best practices and encourage the right actions in salespeople, and in other non-sales functions, to realize consistent sales success.

CPS partner, Mike Higgins, says it best. "The selling organization will be successful only to the extent that the CSO is successful in gaining company-wide commitment of the sales leadership team to a discipline for sales execution. Management discipline is only one of many interconnected factors that determine success, but without this single ingredient, any plans for consistent sales success are not going to happen."

The leadership team itself, however outstanding its members, will not achieve the best results unless they are flying in formation. Sales leaders must demonstrate discipline and predictable rhythm in their actions, and cascade that discipline throughout the customer-facing organization. Management's behavior sends the cultural signals of acceptable behavior.

Discipline and Productivity

If someone asked you what IBM's greatest performance asset has been, what would you answer? People? IBM has always had a raft of outstandingly talented people. But other companies have hired people just as talented. Technology? It has always been good, but not always the best. Many contend that IBM's best performance asset has been its powerful management culture of discipline.

Solid management processes, that were woven into the fabric of the organization, supported IBMers who were belly-to-belly with customers. It was evident in their interactions with customers, each other, their peers, superiors, and partners. Their account leadership and management processes were consistently best-in-class, and were methodically transferred across the company through first- and second-level management. Surprisingly, for years almost none of it was documented. The culture was imbedded in the way leadership acted.

All sales leaders want the selling organization to be a well-coordinated, productive machine that brings great results. Now, that is more of a necessity than an aspiration. Today, most organizations are made up of people from a number of different companies and corporate cultures. The sales environment, as most of them know, is complex and brutal, and everyone has to make every effort count. The CSO and the leadership team need to be doing two things, at the same time.

1. Guide the organization through changes required over time (for example, establish reasonable expectations on the part of the senior management team)

2. Think long-term, but act short-term (for example, produce results while embracing and tuning best practices over time)

They must build for future opportunities and rewards, and consistently deliver near-term wins. They need the same energy, intensity, and focus on best next actions for current and short-term initiatives as for business development for the future. To have even a hope of balancing and achieving these dual objectives, they need to be disciplined and to encourage the same discipline from managers at all levels.

There is another important reason for discipline at the sales leadership level. The current generation of salespeople does not stay in one place very long. These sharp, talented, and highly mobile sales specialists are eager to perform well, but also keen to advance their own skills and value. If they do not follow consistent, disciplined actions directed by the sales leadership team, they are likely to evolve unique selling practices that work for them. These may bring them results in the short term for their own ends, but do not necessarily advance the collective goals of the company and its customers.

Would your sales organization have ready answers if an experienced salesperson joins your group and asks, "What does your sales process look like?

What do you expect from me? How will I be measured?" Because organizational change in most companies and selling organizations is constant and rapid, most CSOs can no longer afford the time for people to figure out how the organization works on their own.

That is true for new *and* incumbent salespeople. Selling organizations need to minimize the amount of calendar time it takes new people to understand their environment and their job—to get *into context*—so that they can apply their experience most productively and quickly to the best next actions that lead to results. One of our client CEOs whose company was on the right slope of a growth curve, was discouraged with the *ramp-up* time for new salespeople. His marching orders were to collapse the time it took to bring on an effective new salesperson. He called it *Day One to Deal Won.*

The sales process definition articulates the "how" we do it. The metrics, review, and discipline keep us on track. The discipline helps salespeople work smarter and mitigate the need for management tirades as the result of disappointing surprises.

A Checklist for Sales Leaders

How does a sales organization know if it has the management discipline that is essential for success? Here are some good questions to ask.

- Is there a standard scorecard or dashboard to regularly assess the progress of opportunities through the pipeline? Does the dashboard include documented customer outcomes? Is it readily visible?

- Is there a calendar in place that triggers management account reviews and pipeline reviews? Or do they pay attention only at the end of a quarter?

- How do sales managers/executives identify the most important things to help salespeople perform beyond expectations? What process is used?

- How effective are sales managers and executives in coaching sales teams to outstanding performance? Does the coaching occur regularly or only sporadically when a big deal is underway?

- Does the management team reinforce the use of selected account management tools by personally using the tools in real account situations?

- Are sales managers disciplined in the way they interact with their clients, ensuring that their role is integrated with the account team, or do they insert themselves only when the deal is in trouble?

If there is a vacuum of discipline in sales leaders' actions, their best intentions will likely be washed away by the waves of daily crises. Our research has identified eight attributes of sales leadership discipline from companies that are themselves best-practice firms.

1. **Customer-focused.** Grounded in desired customer outcomes
2. **Sales-process-based.** Guided by a documented sales process
3. **Intentional.** Requires prescribed actions of customer-facing teams
4. **Developmental.** Promotes relationship and people development
5. **Accountability-driven.** Focuses on what leaders expect and will inspect
6. **Performance-motivated.** Makes clear to teams how their performance is measured and rewarded
7. **Competence-focused.** Emphasizes coaching sales teams at sales process stages
8. **Calendar-driven.** Establishes expectations and follows a timeline

Flying in Formation: Complementary Roles

Successful sales efforts, with rare exceptions, are collaborative endeavors on the part of many talented people. Each member of the company's sales team brings special abilities and expertise to the selling organization. Team members can make contributions to the collective effort based on their own special competence. They will confront challenges that are particular to their role. They have to deliver extremely well within their mandated responsibilities to make the collective effort a success.

The sales team needs to fly in formation—disciplined in their actions and united in purpose. With the right discipline, they can get the same people to produce twice the output. The next section discusses some of the key players and their specialized but critical roles, with key challenges and best practices for each.

The Chief Sales Officer

The CSO is responsible for creating a selling organization that activates corporate strategy for sustainable top-line results. He translates business strategy into a healthy sales pipeline that leads to results. This is the CSO's overall and primary purpose.

The CSO's biggest challenge is to capture the imagination and commitment of the leadership team. To get any real traction, the CSO needs the management team fully enrolled and engaged in the journey of the selling organization. They need common principles and efforts to undertake this journey.

The CSO is part strategist, part team coach. He is the chief morale officer, encouraging the *heart* of selling organization activities. He needs to drive organizational change in the selling organization, as appropriate to selling goals, over time.

His most important task is to declare the intent and the process, and generate enthusiasm for results. He has a sense of urgency for strategic and tactical actions and delivering practical results. This is all about the plan, the actions, and most importantly, accountability.

A great CSO has spirit, lots of heart, and nerves of steel. He needs all these assets as the crucial link between the selling organization and the rest of the company. The CSO's most important capability is to generate and maintain traction for the CSO agenda. He secures support for his agenda from the CEO and other senior management. He delegates authority to first-line sales management to get the job done, while holding them accountable for the implementation of the agenda and results.

Challenges	Best Practices
• Compete with status quo • Buffer *external factors* not under immediate control, but which impact selling organization efforts (competitors, customer business pressures, political developments) • Work well *internally* with people who impact customer-facing activity, but who are not under immediate control • Work well with company senior management to establish realistic expectations and secure resources required • Make this quarter's numbers	• Communicate exciting view of the future and involve sales team in the vision • "Sell" sales agenda to non-sales company executives and managers • Generate sense of urgency around tactical actions and practical results • Hold selling organization leadership accountable for results they are expected to deliver • Measure results and indicators of progress • Celebrate success—recognize achievement and teamwork • Demonstrate personal customer leadership—get engaged and get other executives engaged in critical customer relationships

Chief Executive Officer

The CEO's primary role is to build the value of the company for shareholders and to protect and develop the corporation for the long term. How well this is done affects how well the sales organization can accomplish its objectives. The company's culture, market strategy, value proposition, and operating model are all important to the success of any selling organization. The CSO and the CEO must work in lockstep; the energies of each advance the goals of the other and the company as a whole.

The CEO relies heavily on the CSO to develop overall sales strategy and to identify key initiatives that will move the organization toward its goals. The CSO, in turn, must enroll the CEO as commander-in-chief of the selling organization's objectives, strategies, and initiatives.

Challenges	Best Practices
▪ Be a role model, at the appropriate level, of what is being asked of others	▪ Follow up and touch sales teams; ask appropriate questions, give recognition where it is due
▪ Effectively invest in the resources required to support sales initiatives	▪ Listen hard for signs of difficulty either internally or in the market
▪ Know when to push and when to let people do their jobs	▪ Address indicators in time to maintain course, equilibrium, and momentum
▪ Keep board of directors informed, calm, and supportive	▪ Track progress of initiatives, not to control them but to provide motivation
▪ Commit to and enforce an effective sales communications plan	▪ Reinforce CSO's message to the extended selling team
▪ Keep the organization customer-centric	▪ Regularly discuss sales agenda with customers, operations, and salespeople

Organizational Development Leader/Manager

The organizational development leader is a position that few organizations have in place, but from which many could benefit. It is a role for specifically driving organizational cultural change in directions that increase sales value and value for the company. He partners with the CSO as the CSO's agenda is being socialized and accepted by the company's senior leadership. He can act as a mentor to the CEO and senior executives or take appropriate intervention actions.

Challenges	Best Practices
<ul><li>Get people's attention</li><li>Establish personal and organizational mission's credibility</li><li>Compete with other urgent items on people's agendas</li><li>Get people out of their comfort zone and encourage them to take calculated risks for the sake of corporate objectives</li><li>Get many people, from various functional groups, to walk in the same direction</li></ul>	<ul><li>Get agreement to extraordinary outcomes from senior management</li><li>Get agreement on initiatives to achieve change</li><li>Ensure common understanding of consequences if change not achieved</li><li>Check temperature of initiatives; when they go off course, hold appropriate people accountable</li></ul>

The organizational development leader plants the seeds of ideas and behaviors, and crafts the messages that give momentum to change efforts. She is the stage manager for selling organization activities. She reminds people of their commitments and accountabilities, and asks the tough questions of everyone, at all levels. When problems loom and things get too hot, she is able to calm everyone down and get actions back on track.

Second-Level Sales Manager

The second-level sales manager (for example, vice president of sales for a division) is responsible for having the entire sales organization pulling in the same direction. As division leader, he must have excellent communication skills, be an outstanding leader, mentor, and manager of people, and apply resources fairly and productively. He also needs to have an effective network of leaders from non-sales functions to help achieve selling goals.

As a member of the senior leadership team, the second-level sales manager is responsible for the company's health. Like other leaders at his level, he needs to be concerned about expenses, productivity, and profitability. It is his job to balance corporate and team priorities. He activates the strategy of the CSO.

Challenges	Best Practices
• Assert power to incorporate what is right into the company, despite competition or non-cooperation from senior players who own the resources the team needs • Monitor first-level management activities, have a measurement system in place, and use it to ensure consistent and expected results • Act tough but fair with staff (partner or coach as needed, provide clear objectives, be flexible about how an outcome is achieved, but hold managers accountable for achieving it) • Focus on quality of managers and salespeople; make tough decisions about people (change out poor performers, set the bar higher) • Exercise discretion and good judgment about where to spend time	• Have a communication plan in place and commit to it (ensure staff are committed), and act on it • Take time off the top for key activities: get in front of customers, mentor managers, develop relationships within the company • Demonstrate calendar integrity; always be available when promised • In an emergency or critical situation, drop everything and deal with it • Be consistent about values, criteria, and time to strengthen credibility and relationships, and foster cooperation from others • Make sure actions taken are consistent with corporate and sales organization initiatives

The best second-level managers are consummate translators both up and down the organization. They translate vision into action. They are able to articulate organizational goals into meaningful personal goals. Their perspective encompasses issues facing sales teams and customer and corporate goals, and their actions must reflect both with absolute integrity and clarity.

Sales Manager/Leader

The sales manager is the selling organization's coach, supporter, and activist at the front lines. She needs to garner share of mind for her sales unit from other parts of the selling organization and the rest of the company. She explains the actions of other salespeople and is accountable for the outcome.

The sales manager is closest to the people who do the real work (create value and fill the pipeline). She must generate some quick wins and saves, and keep the teams focused on best next actions. At the same time, she is the key player responsible for executing the sales organization agenda at the customer level. She needs to ensure that best practices become a natural way of working for sales unit staff. Her determination and actions can make or break the selling organization agenda.

Challenges	Best Practices
• Work to have 90 percent of the sales unit executing some best practices all the time through customer-facing team leadership • Filter through mounds of paperwork and process complications to declare larger objectives and best next actions • Protect sales unit from descending into a tactical focus on numbers at the expense of larger strategic and developmental issues • Keep a balance between recognizing extraordinary efforts of individuals and teams, and taking action on unacceptable behaviors and results • Get tough on non-performers by releasing unproductive staff at the right time • Consistently make the numbers	• Touch each sales representative daily/weekly in transaction-focused ways, and in a coaching context • Secure enough resources to support important items, whether crises or opportunities • Hold people accountable for promises and results • Act with complete transparency; explain and discuss any directions, changes, and targets to ensure full understanding and acceptance • Put on the right hat in response to different situations; delegate when appropriate, and take over when needed • Manage pipeline like a corporate asset

Account Manager/Team Leader

The account manager's role is to create high-value, business-to-business relationships with clients that generate a full pipeline of sales opportunities. Many of his responsibilities revolve around business development. The effective account manager is an orchestra leader or quarterback who must coordinate a range of efforts.

He needs to have a steady flow of proactive proposals that meet clients' needs, both within and outside of the normal procurement cycle. The account manager's role also demands a great deal of elasticity, the ability to go the extra mile. He also requires top-notch diplomatic skills within the company to engage subject-matter experts in account initiatives.

The best account managers have a star quality of being able to get *out of the box* to identify customer needs that map to the company's competencies, including innovative value-added items that are exactly what the client needs or can profitably use. He is also responsible for making sure that the client actively recognizes the value that the seller has delivered—before, during, and after delivery.

Challenges	Best Practices
▪ Understand customer organization and business imperatives ▪ Align selling organization resources to customer business problems or pains ▪ Balance strategic selling with short-term business results ▪ Maintain high level of customer satisfaction ▪ Communicate effectively, internally and externally, regarding issues and opportunities related to customer ▪ Apply best resources to most relevant things at the right time	▪ Form outstanding teams around account engagements and generate momentum ▪ Coach everyone working on the account, including non-sales company participants, and recognize successes frequently ▪ Identify key customer initiatives and create appropriate solutions ▪ Create customer value messages that are well understood and repeatable ▪ Promote sense of urgency focused on solving customer problems/issues

Qualities of Disciplined Sales Leaders

We have talked about roles. Now, we will talk a little about qualities and characteristics of strong sales executives and leaders.

Passion. Sales leaders have to make the selling journey exciting and compelling for those who participate in it. People want to spend time where it is exciting, where they stretch themselves to work at the top of their abilities. They also want the energizing rush of results, which leads them to further successes. If everyone can get enthusiastic about possibilities, their journey is lighter and more compelling.

At the same time, sales leaders need to make the playing field as free of obstacles as possible. That means providing guideposts, support, and incentives for those making the journey through disciplined processes and actions. If they know what is expected of them, and what happens when they do or do not do what is required, they can follow the path more clearly and comfortably.

They have passion for their company, their industry, their profession, their team, and mostly, passion for being a problem solver.

Conviction. If a sales leader is not convinced of the merits of his pursuits, he will have little success in persuading others to work with him to fulfill selling organization objectives. Others include the selling organization, the colleagues on whose support and efforts he depends, and the customers he is meant to serve. We believe that sales leaders must have the conviction that *selling organizations exist to help customers to be successful.*

We have found that sales leaders who consistently act on this conviction are always successful over time. This attitude is especially powerful, like invisible armor, for doing battle internally to acquire resources and support needed by the selling organization.

Determination. Good sales leaders are also personally driven by a powerful determination to succeed—in selling outcomes, selling organization credibility and reputation, and selling team satisfaction and development. They are also particularly determined to succeed in advancing customer goals, and achieving customer recognition of the value provided to them. They define their success in terms of customer success.

Determination is important for the sales leader's job for two key reasons. First, the complexity of the job is daunting enough, but at whatever level a leader is operating, there will be difficulties he has to address every day. He needs a steely determination to persevere. Second, because the sales leader's determination is directed toward customer interests, it ultimately serves the selling organization's and company's interests.

Determined sales leaders have confidence based on experience. They have faith in the selling organization's ability to achieve good outcomes because they know enough about right and wrong actions to steer the selling organization and have the resolve to make corrections as warranted.

Stamina and flexibility. Sales leaders need ample supplies of stamina and flexibility. They are agents of change, and they need to make selling activities count where they matter most—with the customers who write the checks.

Selecting top sales agenda items alone requires stamina. Along the way, leaders are likely to face roadblocks and resistance to some initiatives, and the inertia of the way things have been done before. They may face changes in the business environment or in a customer environment, which stalls their plans. They will face daily irritations that undermine progress.

For these reasons, they need flexibility. Everyone has their own needs, their own sense of timing, and of course, their own personal agendas, which can create difficulties for sales leaders. If leaders keep their goals in sight, they can view these situations as small course corrections, but not lose sight of the course.

There is another reason to stay flexible. Sales leaders are continually coordinating not just salespeople's actions, but also those of many players in the company who have particular roles to play in achieving sales objectives.

Chapter Summary

Management rhythm demonstrates predictable, reliable, thoughtful leadership. Sales leaders must cascade discipline throughout their organization so that every level of the organization is flying in formation—disciplined in their actions and united in purpose.

Research-based attributes of sales leadership discipline at best-practices-based companies include these elements.

- Customer-focused
- Sales-process-based
- Intentional
- Developmental
- Accountability-driven
- Performance-motivated
- Competence-focused
- Calendar-driven

The *secret sauce* of sales leadership has a lot to do with the heart as well as the head. The *heart-encouraging* attributes of great sales leaders are passion, conviction, determination, flexibility, and stamina.

13

Create Selling Organization Accountability

The measure of success is not whether you have a tough problem to deal with, but whether it is the same problem you had last year.

—John Foster Dulles

A client of ours recently mused, "What would be the impact on the organization if we had the same level of management discipline for operating expenses as we do for our pipeline and customer assets? We would be out of business!"

This chapter focuses on putting the management discipline we discussed in the previous chapter into action. Some of our clients call this establishing a *management rhythm* or *cadence* for their inspection and coaching rigor.

In many cases, companies invest heavily in educational workshops, bringing cross-functional teams together for account and business planning at the first of the year. Typically in such sessions, participants identify key opportunities and relationship initiatives. While few salespeople like these exercises nor would they volunteer, most appreciate the value and the teams are invigorated as they leave.

There is a flurry of enthusiasm and some action against these plans as people return from the kickoff sessions. The fact that the team has set extraordinary goals will, in itself, lead to business during the year. Some of the teams' relationship actions begin leading to new opportunities. Some of the sales leadership take to heart the commitments to follow up and continue to execute their plan. Things look pretty good.

But for most of these teams, life returns quickly to business as usual within a matter of weeks. Sad, but true. They are doing the same things the same way: responding to problems and low-hanging fruit; spending time with the same people; maybe working harder but not smarter. The strategies and plans they had been so excited about a few months earlier gather dust.

We have all seen this cycle. Sales planning is, in these cases, seen as a one-time event that is tied to start-of-year plans. Things go quietly downhill from there as people wonder what went wrong. How do sales leaders keep the organization moving in the right direction at a steady pace? Micro-managing salespeople is no longer an option.

One of the most powerful ways to keep up momentum in the sales organization and to drive consistent results is to establish a pattern of accountability through regular operational reviews. This keeps the sales force focused on short-term targets that take them toward long-term goals. It also reinforces a culture of accountability in the sales organization, which continues to take participants closer, step-by-step, to the exciting results everyone is seeking.

Accountability—Expectations and Follow-up

Be Clear and Predictable

In countless consulting engagements with well-intentioned sales leaders who introduced change to improve selling organization processes, we found that the lynchpin on which their efforts succeed or fail is the ability to be precise about commitments, requests, and promises (what, when, who).

More often than not, the manager will deliver his requests as a generalized or fuzzy objective, like, "We need to see if we can get some more muscle behind that effort." "Well, sure," say some of the salespeople. Invariably it does not happen—they are not committed to specific actions. The very first thing that sales managers need to do to ensure progress on their team's objectives is to frame their requests clearly, and gain agreement to specific activities, times, contingencies, and review schedules.

The manager's requests for results should be articulated so that salespeople will lay out a path to follow on the way to the target. Sales leaders should clearly frame their expectations, and then follow up on their status regularly. Sales leaders need to back up these words with real oversight and real consequences (positive and negative). They need to *inspect what they expect*, or people will continue to act in inconsistent ways with inconsistent results. They should ask very direct questions.

- What is your goal?
- When do you expect to achieve it?
- What do you need to do to achieve that goal?
- What do you promise to do? By when?
- What are the most important milestones to gauge your progress?
- When would you like to review the results of your actions?

These inspections do not need to be grinding *white glove* inspections. Here are some best practices.

- The conversation should follow a regular, predictable format.
- Sessions should be brief and targeted, with a review of previous commitments and new actions committed.
- Sales managers should ask a lot of why, what, how, and when questions.
- Catch them doing something good! More than half of the discussions should emphasize recognizing doing it right and getting results.
- For every criticism, offer coaching. You should not be calling the plays, but helping them come to actionable conclusions.
- Sessions should be regularly calendared.

Our experience has shown that managers who follow up see more progress than those who do not. This has the effect of reinforcing good practices across the selling organization. If salespeople see a series of quick wins, and if leaders ensure that these are recognized, then the selling organization is well on its way to changing the way it works with customers. Momentum! Traction!

Declare Your Intent

Things change. Team members at all levels often need a wake-up call. In fact, they may need several wake-up calls to get grounded and realize things are not the same. Leaders need to make clear to everyone that there is a disciplined approach to sales activities, and that the organization's livelihood depends on it.

Here is an example of a powerful message to corporate or sales leadership that a CSO or other corporate officer could deliver. In this case, the script is from a COO who is referring to one initiative in his activation of the CSO agenda. Identified by the acronym TEAM (Total Enterprise Account Management), the initiative focused on the company becoming much more customer-centric. How did the COO get the attention he needed for the TEAM effort? He addressed his sales leadership team.

I am not happy with the progress of the TEAM effort.

- I have made a personal commitment to our customers to act as one company.
- I expect us to deliver significant market share growth.
- To achieve these things, I committed to the TEAM effort.
- We have invested $500,000 in this initiative. I expect a return on this investment.
- I do not see any alternative approach that holds as much promise.
- You are in the "hot seat" on this one. You are accountable for sales growth. It is what you get paid for!

The TEAM projects are not something different from your day-to-day selling job. This is your job and I expect you to give it priority.

The COO then outlined what the managers across the corporation needed to do to make the TEAM effort successful.

- I expect you to make a commitment of time and energy to deliver success from this process.
- To ensure that it receives your attention, your chief sales officer and I will have significant input into your performance assessment and compensation.
- I want to be clear that your performance and leadership around the TEAM effort will weigh heavily in my view of future career advancement.

I understand what is happening and I want it to change, as of today. The model for unsuccessful change in our company works like this.

- Someone generates an idea for significant growth within the company.
- The idea gets funded and a process/structure gets put in place to pursue the idea.
- Affected employees recognize that change is required to produce the result, there is mixed support for the idea throughout the organization including the management team (whose personal agendas may be threatened).

- Employees make promises around new behaviors and do not deliver on those promises.
- The process begins to lose steam.
- Efforts to regenerate enthusiasm fail.
- The initiative fails to deliver its promised result.
- Finally, we acknowledge that the process in question does not deliver results.

I am not willing to have this happen to the TEAM process. It is the way we are going to sell in the future.

Therefore, you have a choice. Get behind this effort, deliver on your commitments, and produce results or we will find someone who can.

I know this is blunt, but you have not responded to the coaching and support provided to date. So, I wanted to be very clear with you and make sure that there are no misunderstandings.

Any questions?

If you were an executive or sales leader at this company, how would you feel when you heard this? Got your attention? Senior executive declaration of intent is a necessary first step to establish management discipline, and incorporate accountability—a working, dynamic accountability that infuses all activities—into the selling organization. By itself, however, it is just an opening salvo. Following up with actions that demonstrate you are serious is critical for reinforcing the message.

The Review Process

Regular operational reviews act as a catalyst for maintaining the momentum of sales activities. The review triggers improved sales force management in numerous ways.

- Inspecting progress and performance
- Invoking accountability
- Assessing progress and performance against targets and commitments
- Thanking and rewarding people for success

Operational reviews encourage commitment to accomplishing *important but not urgent* tasks that move them toward milestones and eventually to goals. These continuous in-process check-ups of sales progress lead to right actions by those people who are the subjects of the reviews, at every level. They know the review is scheduled and expect them in the future. They learn to accommodate their day-to-day work with actions to prepare for these periodic, predictable assessments.

In the tumultuous and uncertain nature of business today, operational reviews, at each level for both accounts and opportunities, only happen if they are done *intentionally*. If they are done right, the entire team will begin to act collectively in the same way.

The review process is applicable at all levels. The sales executives should be aiming for *cascading* accountability, assessment, and right actions throughout the sales organization. We will look at actions at each of the following levels to explore how this review process can work.

The Review Process

Level	Incumbent	Accountability
4	Executive management	Measures progress and business unit performance
3	Second-line managers	Accountable for budgets and measuring leading indicators
2	First-line managers	Accountable for quality and currency of plans and attaining milestones
1	Account team leaders	Accountable for taking strategic as well as tactical actions

Next, we will explore an example of this cascading review process from one of our clients.

> The executive management team has assigned global account managers to major accounts, and committed millions of dollars to training and a generous amount of time to implementation. There has been some success and the customers think it is a great idea, but the organization is still lukewarm, unsupportive, and unresponsive. And not just the sales teams, but their executive support teams as well.
>
> The CEO, president, and sales vice president have declared this as a critical success factor for their business—invest in success with our platinum customers. There has been some attention on specific accounts when they pop up as a significant opportunity or there is an obvious problem. A few of these accounts have been able to get traction, but results are spotty. The management committee has the vice president of sales present a simple one-page summary of the top 16 accounts at the

monthly meeting. Everyone expects the scorecard, which includes scoring on the following items, to be presented.

- **Current business results.** Actions leading to clear business results; includes number of orders, revenue, velocity through the pipeline

- **Relationship.** Building and maintaining strong relationships at every level

- **Strategic account management leadership.** Proactive leadership of account and solution initiatives

Review Process Scorecard

Account	Team Leader	Getting it Done	Doing it Right		
		Current Business Results	Relationship	SAM Leadership	Quarterly Value Reviews
SUSTAINED STRATEGIC ACCOUNT MANAGEMENT TRACTION					
Account 1	Grimes	+	+	+	+
Account 2	Wilson	+	+	+	+
Account 3	Bell	+	+	+	+
Account 4	Jones	+	+	+	+
Account 5	Maxwell	+	+	+	+
GETTING STRATEGIC ACCOUNT MANAGEMENT TRACTION					
Account 6	Bland	=	=	+	+
Account 7	Smith	+	−	=	=
Account 8	Marshall	−	−	+	=
Account 9	Morton	=	+	=	=
Account 10	Jackson	+	+	=	=
Account 11	Sims	+	+	=	=
Account 12	Black	=	+	+	+
Account 13	Erickson	=	=	+	+
INTERMITTENT STRATEGIC ACCOUNT MANAGEMENT TRACTION					
Account 14	Grimes	=	−	=	−
Account 15	Stanley	=	=	=	−
Account 16	Pearson	−	−	=	−
− Weak = Mediocre + Strong					

The column for ranking *Current Business Results* corresponds to the Y-axis (Getting It Done) on the Boston box in Chapter 8. The next three columns, *Relationship*, *SAM Leadership*, and *Quarterly Value Reviews* (conducted with the client), correspond to the X-axis (Doing It Right).

Typically, management committee reviews are concerned with corporate operations, staff management, or internal issues. These include recognizing results and people, addressing problems in manufacturing, noting that expenses are too high, or that some parts of the organization are not on board or are struggling.

The kind of scorecard presented here offers a wider perspective that this executive committee cares about. And it is not just for the better appreciation they would gain for the dynamics of successful sales strategies and the real difficulties of executing them. The real benefit of such a review is in *what it causes all of them to do.*

The vice president of sales is well prepared for this meeting. This one-page assessment is not a grinding review, but rather a highlights scorecard. She has a crib sheet of background information on each account that includes such things as biggest results over the month, success in moving account relationships forward, or in moving salespeople toward goals.

At the meeting, conversations are different. They are more focused. As the review unfolds, the executives responsible for good performers will be able to bask in the glow of accomplishments; those with poor performers will be sharpened to attention. Some might question the results (denial), "What do you mean negative relationship development? John told me a few weeks ago he had several meetings lined up!" The vice president of sales replies, "Those were meetings they hoped for. They did not happen." She has the facts to back up her scorecard assessment.

Some might react directly to results. The CEO could be disturbed by poor business results on a particular account because he nurtured this account for years before he became CEO. "This is unacceptable!" he thunders, "I want this fixed!"

This is not just an occasion for some executive members to feel proud and others to feel sheepish. It is an opportunity to air some genuine difficulties and constructive suggestions. "I understand the problems of my people on the Port Industrial account," says one region vice president. "However, I am certain some of these could be addressed through closer cooperation between my account team and Jerry's customer service people." The sales vice president says to the regional vice president, whose account manager finished at the bottom of this assessment, "Jack, I think you should have a word with Charlie about this result. Maybe we should think about finding him a new assignment. This account deserves more from us."

What is really happening at this meeting is a kind of group thinking about *what matters to the account*. The executive committee is focused on how those assessment results impact their business. The review of the scorecard is a way of directing attention to *customer-focused* issues (leading indicators), not just business booked (lagging indicators).

No one in the executive committee wants to see poor results from their own area of influence at the next meeting. They start thinking differently and acting differently, asking pointed and pertinent questions of their subordinates. And those questions will likely be around "getting it done" and "doing it right" because those are the parameters highlighted in the review's summary report. Then, the executives' questions will prompt their subordinates to *drive right actions*. The sales organization will get on board.

What do you think happens after the meeting? Jack, the regional vice president, has a heart-to-heart with Charlie, to try to uncover the reasons for poor traction on the account. From this conversation, Charlie gets the strong impression that if he does not follow Jack's advice and turn things around, he may need to get new business cards. Charlie is motivated to seek out and act out best practices in his areas of responsibility. These follow-up questions and conversations are powerful.

What about the star performers? What an opportunity to recognize those people's achievements! Tom, the Asia-Pacific vice president, goes to Grimes to congratulate him for his excellent efforts, as highlighted in that day's executive meeting. Tom is genuine in his praise. Privately, he thinks he has not done this quite often enough, and makes a mental note to pat people on the back more often. Grimes is pleased, and motivated to keep doing what he has been doing, only better.

Then Tom says, "You know, I am just so delighted with how well you have been handling this account, I am recognizing you with a $2,000 thank you check. I will do that right now. Come with me to my office." Alex, the vice president of North American sales, offers similar accolades to his direct reports, Wilson and Bell, with the same results: even greater motivation to maintain and even exceed their level of achievement. There are now role models for the other sales leads to emulate. Word travels fast.

The teams who are achieving moderate success also benefit from attention after the meeting. This meeting provides an opportunity for executive team members to probe the short-term actions and outcomes, and identify barriers blocking better results. The probing also puts the executive in charge of the account on notice to take some remedial actions himself. The participants can also offer suggestions for pushing modest results to positive ones.

The next management committee meeting is much more productive. Everyone is alert to what is expected, so they ask questions and take actions that will advance those accounts.

We will explore post-meeting issues further as the various review levels are explored in the following paragraphs.

Second-Level Management Reviews

At the beginning of the month, a note from the regional manager's executive assistant advises the 10 branch managers (first-level sales managers) that a regional sales review meeting will be held in 30 days. This will be a *state-of-the-branch* review, which will include *state-of-the-unit* reports from sales managers. The region manager sends out an agenda with templates and timetables to make sure the session is crisp and on point.

- Review results—year-to-date and forecast
- Identify opportunities that will fill the gap
- Identify opportunities that will exceed the goal
- Review one account strategy summary
- Review one opportunity strategy summary
- Review development needs and actions for each group of employees

What if this note from the regional manager, however, also included "Doing it Right" parameters (relationship, strategic account management process, value validation)? Branch managers would likely be thinking before the meeting, "What do I need to ask for or do to be effective at that meeting?"

Instead of scurrying for the same old numbers, these managers would delve into progress on relationships and strategic account management progress.

The conversations will follow a pattern similar to that of the executive meeting conversations. "What is wrong? What can be done about it?" "What is right? How do we capitalize on it?"

Like the executive meeting, there are opportunities for both recognition and redress. More importantly, there are opportunities for guidance and coaching. If an account is just not getting any traction, and it is way behind the schedule that was agreed to, you should schedule a meeting to talk about targeted actions that can be taken to put it back on track, and how you, as a sales leader, can help in that effort.

The biggest impact is on the sales managers in each region. As a result of the review, and the questions from their boss, they begin to think differently about their accounts than they have done to that point. That happens because *their bosses are thinking differently* about the accounts! The manager's questions, guidance, requirements for action, and words of recognition all work to change the thinking and behavior of their subordinates. The questions tie to the strategic account management methodology they all agreed to earlier.

First-Level Management Reviews

This review level is *where the rubber meets the road.* The first-level manager may be responsible for a geographic area, a solution area, or maybe the president of a small business in the enterprise. He is interested in continuously improving performance because he has to be: he is closer to the front lines than the two levels above him. He needs to constantly ratchet up the attention of his subordinates to what is in front of them, and to constantly strive for better actions—more agile and focused actions—to better take advantage of on-the-ground opportunities and make the numbers!

Monthly Reviews

It is critical at this level for the manager to conduct monthly reviews of pipeline activities and progress with sales managers. These are short, crisp meetings designed to minimize office time and maximize time to sell. It is also a good practice at this level to conduct win-loss reviews, as these are appropriate. Where warranted, a smart first-line manager also carries out on-the-spot reviews of specific sales situations.

The emphasis at this level is largely tactical, and the questions targeted. "What is the situation on this account or opportunity? What is the best thing to do next? What else can we do to keep the Scully Steel account? Has anyone talked to Sam about the status of the industry standard development initiative?"

The first-level manager's role is to provide direction and offer help. "What should we do to firm up the Nexus opportunity? Now, I will have to work out something with Sam in product development to move his development along. I will make sure I get the resources you need on that McLaren deal. We also need marketing to be on board with this, so I will line that up with John as soon as I can."

Top-Five Reviews

One of the most useful review exercises that can occur at this level is a weekly conference call to review critical sales situations and ensure that adequate and appropriate resources are applied where needed. First-line managers can outline what they consider critical issues or top opportunities.

This is a way of getting everyone focused on developments that can have the greatest impact on the group's success. There are two other very important functions of these conference calls. One is that the first-line manager can offer to provide specific kinds of help to sales managers to advance their objectives. "What can I do to help you achieve that?" is a powerful message from the first-line manager to build credibility and get commitment to actions that enable results.

Secondly, these regular sessions enable first-line managers to transfer best practices to others on critical issues raised in the call. They can draw on their own experience and on knowledge gained from review exercises in which they participate with their boss.

As a result of issues raised in these *top-five* calls, certain targeted *war room* discussions might ensue. For example, a large opportunity may have significant ramifications, making it necessary to plan appropriate actions and coordinate them. It is in these sessions that participants make promises to each other (and the boss) about what actions they will undertake.

The promises are recorded so that everyone knows what to expect at the next stage of the initiative.

Team Leader/Global Account Manager Reviews

The difference between a sales manager at this level and an account manager is reporting relationships. While the sales manager works primarily with people who report to him, the team leader or global account manager works mainly with people who do not. Both, however, have similar obligations to stay on top of activities and events in their own area of responsibility.

Good sales managers make a point of conducting weekly reviews of progress on volume and velocity of pipeline accounts and opportunities, work plans for critical sales opportunities, best next actions to promote relationship initiatives in key accounts, and opportunities for coaching incumbents on tricky situations.

Global account managers also benefit from regular discussions of work plans for key sales opportunities and account relationship initiatives. However, their discussions take place with other solutions, product, or service line managers and non-sales personnel. The practice of targeting best next actions, making commitments and securing commitments from partners, and tracking progress apply equally to this more delicate domain of activity.

With no direct reports assigned, the global account manager needs all the diplomacy and best practices he can muster to enroll others in customer-related strategies, make requests for actions by others, overcome roadblocks, and hold people accountable to their promises.

Functional Review Sessions

Another less structured way to achieve the benefits of operational reviews is to conduct regular review sessions with functional interest groups. This could be a monthly team leader meeting or a session over dinner with global account managers, product/service line managers, or customer service managers. They can discuss issues and ideas with each other, their boss, and with a high-ranking executive to whom they do not report.

These sessions have the effect of educating participants on key issues, transferring best practices, and presenting role models for others to emulate. They also encourage an informal bonding (enrollment) among interest group participants.

As long as these are considered valuable to the participants, the customer and the selling organization, frequent events of this kind in the sales organization help to form a tighter and better performing organization—with better focus, better practices, and as we will see, better results.

The Amazing Power of Reviews

Here are some key characteristics of powerful operational reviews.

- **Format.** Short, consistent parameters, regularly scheduled, fact-based
- **Function.** To recognize progress and to drive accountability through the selling organization
- **Technique.** Ask good questions, gain insight
- **Result.** Improved short-term actions

Operational reviews can change everybody, with management asking better questions and people closest to the customers supplying the answers. Done right, this forces people to think early in terms of best next actions. The following personal story taught the author that the review exercise is not about what people upwards need to know, but what people *downwards* need to do to move account activity forward.

A number of years ago I was promoted from a sales manager job to a regional staff manager for IBM. My boss, Les Lesniak, had responsibility for 10 branches covering three states, with 500 sales and sales support professionals who generated $1 billion per year in revenues. One of my duties was to facilitate the branch review process for the year. I designed the review formats and went with him to the on-site reviews.

Although I had taken part in reviews over the years, as a field salesperson and sales leader, I had never had this perspective. I designed what I thought was a great review format, communicated this to the branches, and set up the schedule: ten half-day branch reviews over a two-week period.

At each branch meeting, the branch manager handed Les a beautiful bound book of their reviews. I took a copy of each of them, along with my notes, back to our regional office. I assumed that we would then take the data, consolidate it, analyze it, come to some conclusions, and forward this analysis to our division headquarters.

During the reviews, I noticed that Les was not taking many notes (he only wrote down things he had promised he would do and a list of some of their commitments for follow-up), while I was trying frantically to capture all of the relevant information not in their written documents. When we returned, I took a copy of all 10 branch reviews into his office and said, "Les, what do you want me to do with these?"

He took them, threw them in the trash and said, "Art, these reviews were not for me. They were for them. If I had not requested the reviews, they would not have stepped back and looked at their accounts and territories as a business. Many of them would not have done the things they should have been doing anyway. This is one of the critical ways I get these wild ducks to fly in the same direction, and I need to do this several times a year."

At each level, the operational review is guided by the one at the level above it, and reinforces the directions of the one below it. The cascade effect of everyone in the sales organization anticipating the next review and acting accordingly creates a very disciplined sales organization—one in which everyone is focused on actions that produce consistent results. What happens at levels *above* and *below* every review?

Effects Below

People do not like to be put on the spot and assessed on their performance. It is human reluctance to be called out and, in many cases, there is a fear of failure. People do not have to like operational reviews to appreciate the value of those reviews—for the benefit of the unit, for the benefit of the sales organization, and especially for the *positive* effect of those reviews on their own work performance and career.

As a result of being asked to take certain actions in preparation for a review, the "reviewee" begins to take those actions themselves. They take the actions because they know how to do so, and it saves being embarrassed the next time. Then an amazing thing often happens. They begin to see improved results from these sales activities.

The account manager gradually comes to appreciate the value of right actions for his own sales activities, and falls into the habit of taking different actions for an opportunity or account. He has deeper and better relationships with customers, has a better understanding of their needs and how to help them make money, has more orders, higher revenue results, and moves his sales opportunities through the pipeline faster.

Effects Above

Consider the top level, the executive committee. The members of the executive committee are themselves conditioned to ask more consistent and better questions. They learn to think not just about getting it done, but also about doing it right. Their focus, in turn, affects the leaders at the next level, and the next ones. Another important thing happens. By doing the review, they may discover ugly blemishes in the business, and take on accountability to repair them—in time!

Now, all members of the sales organization are playing complementary roles to everyone else. They are working to keep the organization either humming in good times or surviving profitably in bad times. Sales leaders get a sales organization that is on top of all issues, not just when a deal is in front of them, but always. Because of this process, they avert many problems, seize new opportunities, and more effectively respond to unforeseen issues.

From Team Accountability to Individual Development

When sales leaders follow up on commitments made by salespeople for specific actions, significant benefits accrue to the leaders, the salespeople, and the selling organization. Leaders may have to spend time checking on progress, but they save themselves a lot of pain. Salespeople begin to have more successful outcomes, which increase their confidence in their abilities. They take themselves to the next level, and make more money.

The interventions that occur during reviews should be seen and treated as a form of coaching. The next chapter shows how coaching, sales leadership development, and effective compensation practices serve as important bookends to spur individual performance.

Chapter Summary

How does a sales leader predictably manage the selling organization to accountable actions and results? A predictable, calendared review process is informational for the entire organization. An organized and brief review can be energizing, and can quickly and repeatedly encourage behavior as well as results. It also provides coachable moments.

Reviewing results is important; reviewing commitments to action is critical! A good review must include an evaluation of the sales opportunity pipeline. It must drive the people who are presenting it to step back and take a look at their territory like a businessperson.

The review process should cascade in the organization from the executive team to the customer-facing teams so that everyone is flying in formation.

14

Coach and Compensate Sales Teams for Results

When I was very young, my father used to tell me that an army of deer led by a lion will defeat an army of lions led by a deer. At Duke, Coach Krzyzewski was our lion.

—Grant Hill

Our customers today are very different than they were in the good old days. The business environment is much less predictable. Team selling is one of the most successful models we see our clients employ to deal with this new environment. Teams need support and development, including coaching, not directive micro-management.

Sales teams are constantly reinventing themselves to align with their customer's environment. When they are at their best, they are in sync with the customer's tactical and strategic initiatives. But the best actions that need to be taken are sometimes not clear. The coach helps these teams gain their bearings. The sales manager's coaching skills are critical.

Salespeople usually respond most intensely to satisfying others' expectations—their leaders', the customers', the company's—as well as their own goals for themselves. With coaching, sales leaders can keep them on track by giving them advice and resources when required and recognizing their achievements along the way.

An effective sales review process raises visibility of the accounts, opportunities, issues, and people that need attention. A clearly defined sales process sets up valuable moments for sales leaders to coach salespeople and teams to be more productive, efficient, and successful. Coaching sales teams helps them establish goals to work toward, and at the same time, the discipline they need to work smarter.

Seizing coachable moments that surface through normal activities of a sales process gives sales leaders their chance to provide effective coaching. The coached salesperson improves the selling organization's performance, and will improve their odds of success because their confidence and esteem improve.

Coaching: Learning from the Best

The bedrock of good coaching is the value of learning from the best. It is a principle that serves both sales leaders and selling teams. The sales coach can effectively transfer peak performance throughout the selling organization. The salespeople can accelerate their success through learned insights and focused skill development. Consider this perspective from the author.

> The subject of large-account-selling best practices has intrigued me for over 30 years, ever since the day my IBM branch manager, Dick Haar, told me, to my surprise, that I was going to be a salesperson rather than a systems engineer, the job for which I had been hired. Although being in sales gave me a great deal of anxiety, it was better than the alternative: no job at all.
>
> In the first meeting with Bill Barley, my new sales manager, he asked me how I felt about the job. I told Bill that I was excited. Actually, I was petrified. I asked for his suggestions about getting started, surviving, and excelling. He suggested that I find salespeople who were most successful, then identify and adapt their best practices to my style.
>
> What I found was that these best-of-breed salespeople did only a few things differently, but had substantially higher results. The best tended to do 50 to 100 percent more business than the average salesperson.
>
> My anxiety paid off. The coaching I requested and received from many outstanding sales leaders and clients inspired me to implement many successful practices that I would have missed otherwise. I have made a point of continuing this quest for the best coaching over my career.
>
> When I became a sales team leader, I was able to pass along these gifts by coaching others. The proof is always in the results: Many customers recognized my selling teams as high-value partners, and my employers saw them as generators of high-value results. Ultimately, I

found that these lessons could be translated into consistent coaching habits.

Four Coaching Habits

Since 1992, CPS has been developing a set of coaching tools that help selling teams create and manage strategies for large accounts, complex sales opportunities, and key relationships. We also identified four habits for effective coaching in a chapter we wrote for a book by Robert Hargrove, *Masterful Coaching Fieldbook* (San Francisco, CA, Jossey-Bass/Pfeiffer, a Wiley Company, 2000). Of course, there are many factors that make up an effective coach. A great resource is *Coach Anyone About Anything* by Germaine Porché and Jed Niederer (Del Mar, CA, Wharton Publishing, Inc., 2001).

We have seen these four critical habits produce breakthrough results for selling teams. We have also identified for each a *best practice* for becoming a world-class coach. These are the four key coaching habits that we identified.

1. Establish high-value coaching relationships
2. Identify coachable moments
3. Help teams develop extraordinary goals
4. Get commitment to actions

Coaching Habit 1. Establish a High-Value Coaching Relationship

Whether the coaching relationship is requested by the player (the person being coached) or by the potential coach, it is very important that this relationship (and the act of coaching itself) be clearly separated from any other, pre-existing relationship. It is different. If it is not different, the conversations will quickly revert back to the previous relationship.

Also, it should be a cardinal rule of every coach to *ask permission* to give coaching, *every time*. A player who has given permission to be coached will always be more receptive. Without permission, the coaching runs the risk of perceived telling, directing, or preaching. The player will back up. Here is an example.

> Recently, we observed a meeting with a salesperson and her manager. She (the salesperson) was responsible for one of the company's largest customers. She was very emotional and was loudly complaining about the situation with her customer and asked for her manager's advice. However, every time her manager tried to interject an observation, she would complain more loudly.

He finally decided just to let her talk, and after a few minutes he asked her if she wanted him to coach her. She sat back, paused, took a deep breath, and said yes. He then asked her a few questions. They quickly found what was missing and developed some short-term actions that might correct the situation. Before the manager offered the coaching, he was just a vehicle for letting off steam. After the offer, he became a partner in solving the problem.

An effective way to establish a good coaching relationship is to share your coaching philosophy with the player and be true to it. These are the things a good coach does.

- *Listens hard!* Coaching is a conversation, not an interrogation.
- *Offers and suggests*, rather than tell and dictate. Mutual trust is extremely important.
- *Asks thoughtful questions*. Count to five slowly before interjecting.
- Helps the player find out *what is missing* to move forward.

If the coach is not the manager, we recommend that an actual coaching *contract* be set up. It should cover basic ground rules, expectations, and scheduling time. However, in the field of large-account sales, a coach and player may find it difficult, if not impossible, to stick to a regular schedule for coaching sessions, particularly if the coach is also the manager. Things come up, the most urgent of which are customer- or competitor-driven. Therefore, we have found it valuable for the coach to look for coachable moments. These are moments in which the player will be particularly receptive to being coached (habit #2).

Best Practice 1. Create a Trusted Coaching Relationship

Establish a coaching relationship even when it is not easy and is not comfortable. Sales leaders should focus their coaching energy on enrolling and engaging players who need them the most. Many clients and other players who later became some of our best friends were very difficult people in the beginning, but we persisted in developing a coaching relationship with them.

In the book, *Trusted Advisor* (Maister, Green, and Galford. New York, NY, Touchstone, 2000), the authors put forth an intriguing model that we find applicable to coaching.

$$\text{TRUST} = \frac{\text{Reliability} + \text{Credibility} + \text{Intimacy}}{\text{Self-Orientation}}$$

The coach must be trusted to ensure success. To build trust, the coach must convince the player that he is reliable, credible, and understands the player's environment. The player must also believe that the coach is in it for the player, not the coach.

Coaching Habit 2. Identify Coachable Moments

How can a coach tell when a coachable moment may be in front of him? Here are some signals you may hear from the player.

- Do you have a minute?
- There is something I would like to run by you.
- What would you do in a situation like this?
- I am stuck.
- By the way...

The ideal signal that a player is coachable is the player saying to the coach, "I would really appreciate your coaching on something." The best coaching is coaching that has been requested.

> It was a dark and stormy night. The branch manager packed up her briefcase, turned out the lights and headed out. Her top account executive was burning the midnight oil preparing for a presentation that will make his year. The workspace was piled with three ring binders, charts, and lots of coffee cups. She wished him well and he replied, "Chief, I am mired in so much detail, I cannot get the creative juices going. Unless I have a breakthrough, we will be toast tomorrow." She offered her help. He accepted. She asked him to visualize the five people in the room. What did he want them to individually say after his presentation tomorrow? What questions did he want them to ask? After a 15-minute discussion, he said, "I have it! Thanks!"

A key to discovering coachable moments is *being there*, that is, being centered on the player, not on one's self as coach. We have found that many coachable moments occur before or after operations reviews and at critical stages of the sales process.

Best Practice 2. Coach for an Impending Event

The best practice for finding coachable moments is to look for those instances when large-account salespeople are planning an important and tough customer call. There is anxiety that can be refocused to energy and creativity.

We have found that the following questions will typically yield several times the impact of normal call preparation.

- When you walk out of the room, what is it you want the customer thinking?
- What are your most important two or three objectives for the meeting?
- What are two or three key customer needs we could satisfy during this meeting?
- What are the two or three questions we could ask that would have the highest impact in helping us achieve the objectives of the call?
- What would be the best two or three openings we could use that would get the call off to the best possible start?

Coaching Habit 3. Help to Set a Specific Extraordinary Goal

Nothing inhibits right actions by salespeople and team members more than not having a defined goal and a target date for completion. Without a goal, selling teams are destined to spend most of their time focused on the urgent rather than on the important. Without a defined goal, even the most skilled professional selling team members will wander in the desert looking for the oasis. Selling team members who are part-time on the project will lower the priority for this project as part of their share of mind and actions. They do not like to wander.

We all know that having goals is very important, but in selling situations most professionals will avoid setting specific goals with dates. Why? In our subconscious, we believe that if we set a clear goal and a deadline, we have set ourselves up for potential failure. Experience shows, however, that those who set specific goals have significantly higher success rates.

> The account executive we discussed earlier knocks on the branch manager's door and smiles. "How did it go," she inquires. "Good news! They signed up. Thanks for the coaching last night! Bad news? I am not sure our dog will hunt. I am a little foggy on how to get over the finish line. In fact, I am unclear about where the finish line is. How about helping me get the target in sight?" She congratulates him on the results of the meeting. She says this is a great problem to have. "We will start with what the customer would describe as extraordinary and go from there."

There are five aspects to setting goals that we believe are important.

1. What is it that will be recognized by the customer as extraordinary value?

2. Validate

3. Socialize with your team to get the extraordinary goal in sight

4. Carve up the goal into milestones—we know we are there when…

5. Put the milestones into accountabilities and execute like your life depends on it

We recommend that the coach always ask the person (or team) to state clearly and openly (penalty free) the goals to be achieved. The next great question is to articulate the benefit to the customer, should we realize our goal. To get the goal to *have energy*, ask these questions.

- What are the specific products and services that we would like the customer to buy from us? When could they commit?

- How can we articulate the value of our recommendation in customer terms? Who needs to concur with the value proposition?

- What kind of relationship do we need to have from the customer's perspective in order to get these results? By when?

- What are the best next actions that we need to take?

Best Practice 3. Set a Goal Based on Customer Success

What is the best practice for setting the goals? Think big from the customer's point of view. Here is a personal example from the author. His first sales partner, Jeff Pace, a great coach and role model, took a lot of interest in his success.

> Our major account was a large city government, and Jeff assigned me to sell to the city hospital. At the time, computers were primarily used only for back-office accounting functions. Being anxious to succeed quickly, my obvious focus was to sell a new medium-sized system to move the processing for the back-office accounting from the city's central computer system to a new system in the hospital.
>
> I was very excited about this sales opportunity and asked for Jeff's advice. He got me to step back and take a longer-term look from the customer's view. He suggested that if we could get the customer to see the long-term value of automation of the whole hospital, our odds of success on the first phase would be higher, and the medium- to long-term business would be much easier to sell.

And that is exactly what happened. The initial part of the sales process did take a couple of months longer, but in the end the client sole-sourced the business to us, the commitment was for a longer term, our revenue was five times larger, and because of the linkage to their business needs, emphasis on successful implementation was across the entire organization. The client's measured return showed less than a two-year payback on the entire capital investment, and we supplied that customer with its key computer needs for over a decade—all because of a great coach!

I have personally experienced and studied the phenomenon of the importance of thinking big for over 30 years as a player and as a coach. I know that using a coach (whether a manager, team leader, consultant, or customer) to help identify an extraordinary goal increases the overall business opportunity significantly. By using a coach, you increase the value to the client, the revenue to the selling company, and the odds of winning.

Coaching Habit 4. Gain Commitment to Action

Why is it so important for the coach to gain commitment to best next actions in a selling environment? Unlike normal project planning, strategies in complex selling environments are built with only limited knowledge of all the facts.

Because, frequently, how best to achieve the goal is a little foggy, as a guideline, sales leaders should not try to get long-term committed actions from team members, but rather get commitment to the goal and some agreed-to milestones along the way. Crisply executed short-term, best next actions related to the milestones help gain momentum and build enthusiasm toward reaching the goal.

Here is another story from the author.

> After a number of years of success as a salesperson, I was promoted to lead a number of salespeople in a territory composed of large medical center hospitals and hospital chains. This territory had been a sales disaster for several years. The technical support people and young salespeople who survived these difficult times were excellent professionals, but in the dumps.
>
> During the first year, I set and managed strategies for all key accounts and for major sales opportunities, and directed the actions of all team members. I noticed over time that, although everyone agreed to my strategies during the planning sessions, people seemed to be waiting

around for me to take action or to tell them what to do. And as hard as I worked, I could not handle and direct all the active strategies. As a result, the second year was one of the worst business volume years in the history of that territory and my career.

In fact, my job was on the line and I asked for some coaching from my new sales manager, Scotty Walsh. He gave me one year to turn it around, and some excellent advice, "Art, you are a great personal salesman, but you cannot do everything. You have some people working with you who have incredible potential, but they cannot grow and really contribute if you direct them in every strategy and action. If you do not move into more of a coaching role with the other salespeople, you will not make it." That got my attention!

My role changed from chief salesman to strategy facilitator and coach. I learned the value of stepping back and helping others create their extraordinary goals, customer-centric selling strategies, and work plans that consisted of a small number of milestones and short-term, written, committed actions.

After that was done, it was a matter of reviewing these strategies and work plans regularly. There was a continuous team focus on short-term actions that supported the key strategic goals for each client. As a result, for five years this team sold more business each year than had been sold in the previous five years combined!

Best Practice 4. Commit to Best Next Action

Combined with a rhythm of coaching, the following best practices gain commitment to action and transfer from coach to the team.

- Frequent, crisp conversations on where we are and what each person will do next
- Commit time to accomplish best next actions
- Communicate results of actions

The Coaching Payoff

The highest-impact selling organizations of the future will be made up of relatively few selling professionals and many others who will focus on, develop, and execute customer-centric selling strategies for major customers, complex selling opportunities, and key relationships. They will manage these strategies and the virtual teams that execute the work plans as projects. The payoff from coaching is getting the work done! There is no alternative.

David Ernsberger, former vice president of sales for the IBM Storage Technology Group, took the OEM disc drive business which, although based on leading-edge technology, was not profitable nor well known in the marketplace to spectacular success with an inexperienced sales staff. In five years, the business grew from two percent to 15 percent of market share, and was more profitable than all its competitors combined—one of IBM's most impressive profit-generating lines of business during the late 1990s.

Over this time, Dave generated fierce loyalty and high performance among his sales managers, who were instrumental in his success. Dave recruited or developed the following qualities in his sales management team.

- Unwavering focus on winning: customer insight, breakthrough thinking, drive to achieve
- Ability to mobilize a team to execute: team leader, straight talk, teamwork, decisive
- Ability to sustain momentum: organizational capability, strong coach, personal commitment
- Passion for the business and the business of selling: do whatever it takes to advance the company

Dave's success was based on both leadership and management best practices. Passion and focus on winning are the marks of a leader who can drive the selling organization toward outstanding performance. Mobilizing teams and building organizational capability are management attributes to keep operations moving smoothly.

How is this caliber of leadership management and coaching developed, encouraged, and promoted? According to Dave, there are three important steps for sales leaders to take to cultivate high-quality sales leadership and management.

Know the business. Make sure that sales managers know the fundamental principles of their company's business—and know them to the core of their being—and correspondingly understand their particular role in serving and advancing the business. This is a gesture of respect towards those managers. It says, "I believe that you have the intelligence and commitment to serve this organization well, and I want to make sure you are clear about the organization's business and way of doing business."

Clearly define expectations. Make absolutely clear to managers what is expected of them, collectively and individually, especially minimum expectations. This, too, is giving them the advantage of clarity and the support of discipline to help them execute their responsibilities well.

Offer solid support. It is particularly important to let sales managers know, unequivocally, that when they find themselves on thin ice, they can and should ask for help. They must always have the option to go to the next level for assistance on difficult issues. It should be made clear that no negative perceptions will be attached to such actions. However, managers must also know that executive management will view charging ahead without asking for support when warranted, unfavorably. The message: no surprises!

Managing Salespeople for Mutual Benefit

Outstanding sales leaders are particularly astute in drawing out the best abilities, skills, and special talents of team members. These talents will be different, of course, but each of them is individually useful to the collective goals of the group.

Many sales leaders have said that managing salespeople is sometimes like herding cats. They recognize that salespeople have characteristics that are different from those of other professionals in a company. What is it that makes many managers believe that sales professionals require special handling?

They are isolated and independent. They usually work alone or in small virtual teams. They do need feedback and attention, and the sales manager is usually their first line of support. Most of them have gravitated to sales because they like the freedom to do their own thing.

They are in a glass cage. Gaps between management's expectations and their performance are easily measurable and visible. Customers also have expectations and are quick to point out disappointments.

They are boundary spanners. They interface with a lot of people to get the job done. They negotiate between the customer and the business.

They are constantly stressed. They face pressure from everywhere all the time—customers, competitors, management, and the banks. They take the heat when the company's products or services fall short.

Not surprisingly, managing salespeople is often quite a task. Their unique ways of working and the constantly shifting sales environment make the sales manager's job particularly challenging. What he has to do is to inspire, manage, and support a team of well-trained, highly motivated people to consistently make their numbers. In the fast-paced world of selling where the manager seldom sees his salespeople, what does it take to do this?

In an article in Sloan Management Review (Vol. 34, No. 3), *Transforming the Salesforce with Leadership*, the authors (Marvin A. Jolson, Alan J. Dubinsky, Francis Yammarino, and Lucette B. Comer) explore the premise that, in the specialized area of personal business-to-business selling, a combination of transactional and transformational leadership is required to help salespeople and sales teams achieve better results. Transactional leadership deals with day-to-day actions; transformational leadership is focused on behavior management.

Transactional leadership is familiar to most sales leaders. Management establishes an agreement with the salespeople, formally or informally, that reinforces a desired behavior. For example: *If you accomplish X, you will get Y, and if you do not accomplish X there will be repercussions.*

The Sloan article cites one sales manager who had a sign on his desk stating: *No Orders, No Money.* While many sales professionals are drawn to the "money for orders" approach, it does not always work, especially for less-experienced salespeople. Less-seasoned workers can become quickly disillusioned and find another sales job or quit sales altogether.

With transactional leadership, management by exception is the rule, and it works for both parties. Experienced sales managers and competent salespeople tend to gravitate toward transactional leadership. Salespeople want executive management to set goals for them and deliver the rewards when goals are achieved. They want to have suggested methods for achieving goals, and to know what inspection will occur.

Transformational sales leadership augments the transactional style. It focuses on the salesperson's personal and professional aspirations to connect these desires with current and required actions. Here are some attributes of this style.

Passion. Transformation leaders inspire their team with an assertive approach that demonstrates confidence and encourages risk-taking. They act out what they want to see. They empower the salespeople to do the right thing. They generate energy.

Intellectual stimulation. Transformational leaders develop a readiness for change in salespeople. They encourage new thinking, innovative approaches and behaviors. They connect the company's business strategy with the salesperson's personal strategy.

One-on-one approach. Salespeople in any selling organization have different strengths and weaknesses, training needs, territories, and results. Successful sales leaders pay attention to these differences. They capitalize on strengths and improve weaknesses in each individual. They work on preventative measures, not just remediation.

In our experience, best-practices-driven selling organizations recognize and leverage the unique qualities that each sales team member brings to the job. When a company can take advantage of this diversity, it enables sales teams to accomplish extraordinary results.

Sales managers also have special characteristics and bring particular skills and insights to their job. We believe that a healthy mix of management styles can be of great benefit for developing a highly effective sales organization, but clearly coaching skills are at the top of the list.

We often see selling organizations in which certain management styles are encouraged to the exclusion of other complementary styles. Although management styles need to fit the culture of a company, we believe that having sales managers who show both a combination of transactional and transformational leadership will lead a sales organization to greater levels of success and accomplishment.

Some Thoughts about Compensation

Another management tool to motivate the right behavior is compensation. However, it should not be the only tool.

Here are some criteria for a compensation plan to work well in a selling environment.

Visibility. The plan needs to be absolutely clear to everyone, well-articulated, and based on credible metrics. If leaders are not upfront about how people are rewarded, they will break the important psychological contract they have with salespeople.

Performance-driven. The plan should be performance-driven and not seen as a kind of entitlement of role or position. The plan should encourage the top 50 percent of the sales force to go after the top business initiatives in the marketplace. The plan effectively becomes skewed to outstanding performance. This can encourage the change in sales culture that produces extraordinary results.

Reward excellence. Make sure that those who really excel in their work also excel in their paychecks. In fact, the best compensation schemes for salespeople are designed so that outstanding performers are justly compensated at levels equal to or exceeding senior sales executives in the company. If this is done for salespeople who turn in an awesome performance over the year, it is a signal to the whole selling organization that its most important job is to go belly-to-belly with customers.

Broad recognition of ability. A good compensation scheme also recognizes the mix of an individual's past and current contribution to the firm. In other words, someone who is a consistently good performer over time has more opportunity to perform even better and earn even more.

Consistency. Good sales compensation plans have some similarity between its components and those of the management compensation plan. People will quickly lose their commitment to the sales mission if they see their hard work rewarded one way, and the work of management compensated completely differently.

> One of our client executives was unhappy about results. Her staff presented various theories about what was not working, but she was still unhappy. She decided to conduct roundtables with front-line salespeople so she could get closer to reality, their reality.
>
> In each of these roundtables she stood up, put her hand over her heart and swore she would not be offended by any criticism, especially if it was a constructive one. After the chuckles, the dialogue began to flow. A consistent theme was that the compensation system was driving behavior that was out of sync with the customer's buying and decision-making process. It rewarded people for doing non-customer-centric things.
>
> She enrolled one volunteer from each of the seven roundtables onto a task force to revamp the compensation model. She set forth the following principles for the team to work under.
>
> - Success with customers will translate to our company's success and will yield commensurate rewards to the sales team members
> - Simplicity in design and implementation
> - Sustainable for at least three years
> - High rewards for share of customer wallet growth
> - Tie compensation of management team to sales teams
>
> The task force was skeptical at first but the energy began to flow. A compensation system was developed in a customer-balanced scorecard format. It was accepted and piloted on two teams from each of the seven task forces. After six months, each of these teams was outperforming their peers.

Chapter Summary

Effective coaching builds competency from the ground up, and can effectively transfer peak performance throughout an organization. Coaching relationships that hum have important features. They establish the relationship, identify coachable moments, set goals, and get commitment to action.

Salespeople are in unique positions with unique individual coaching needs. Coaching sales teams requires more focus on transformational leadership rather than transactional leadership. This leadership style focuses on creating opportunities for salespeople to deliver results to their companies as well as deliver on their personal and professional aspirations.

Leaning on a compensation program alone will not be effective in motivating a selling organization. For a compensation plan to work well, it needs to have visibility throughout the organization, be performance-driven, reward excellence, and recognize ability over time.

Epilogue

When I began my professional career as a systems engineer in 1969, I had no idea that I would ever go into sales. And I certainly did not think that decision would lead to writing this book. But throughout my career, I found the success of One-Percenters an intriguing subject. How do these people produce four and five times the business of the "average" salesperson? Ultimately, I would make their field-proven operating practices the foundation for Critical Path Strategies' intellectual property and consulting practices.

Throughout the years, people have asked, "Why Critical Path Strategies? Why did you select that name for your consulting company?"

Observing extremely successful salespeople and their leadership, I was struck by how similar their thought process is to the mathematical basis for *critical path analysis*. It must be the engineer in me! That process, whether applied to complex mathematical problems, engineering projects, or business situations, helps people identify the best, actionable, short list of important things that must be accomplished to achieve their goal. The CPS technique of applying this solution to the sales environment helps sales leaders and their teams methodically create a goal, and a strategy to achieve that goal, in a way that connects personal accountability directly to strategy-related actions.

This *critical path* thought process produces a way for sales leaders and their teams to consistently identify, develop, activate, and maintain the momentum of selling strategies that focus on the customer. Consistent use of the conversation that creates a critical path changes the behavior of the people in the organization and the customer in a way that significantly improves the results for all of the stakeholders. Our clients find that it leads to extraordinary outcomes.

Why is this important? Most of our clients know that they cannot depend upon One Percenters to carry the team. They need the rest of the selling organization to take actions that replicate the outcomes that One Percenters generate naturally.

What would I recommend to sales leaders? Over the years, I have asked scores of successful sales leaders the following question, "As you reflect on the leadership positions you have held during your sales career, what would you have done differently?" Consistently, the answer resembles, "I would have run the right play sooner!"

About Critical Path Strategies, Inc.

Since its formation in 1992, CPS has counseled sales leadership and sales teams in over 100 global corporations. By transferring its best-practices-based sales team framework to client sales teams, CPS enables clients to build high-value relationships, expand sales opportunities, improve sales productivity, increase sales team confidence, and grow top-line revenue. CPS clients regularly measure 100 to 500 times their CPS investment in revenue growth by developing strong, global selling organizations, and activating customer-focused initiatives that are scalable, efficient, and repeatable.

CPS Offerings

- **Executive Planning** for key members of executive leadership teams is designed to assess, select, and prioritize critical initiatives required to create sustainable revenue growth.

- **CSO Agenda** enables sales leaders to assess, select, prioritize, and rapidly implement critical initiatives required to create sustainable revenue growth.

- **Sales Process Optimization** aligns the selling organization's processes and methodologies with customer needs and expectations through in-depth review of the organization's strategy, supporting technology, people, and processes.

- **Account Management Execution Assessment** helps sales leaders assess their selling organization's performance against documented best practices in managing key accounts.

- **Value Message Alignment** helps sales teams align high-level value propositions with customer-specific business issues.

- **Strategic Account Management** helps sales teams develop customer-centric account strategies and actionable plans for strategy execution.

- **Relationship Management** brings stakeholder groups together to establish or enhance collaborative relationships with key customers, partners, suppliers, dealers/channels, inter-company departments, and cross-company businesses.

- **Sales Leadership Team Coaching** adds dimension to sales-based or strategic company initiatives.

Representative Client List

Acxiom Corporation
ARCADIS NV
Bell Microsystems
BindView Corporation
BMC Software, Inc.
Candle Corporation
Caterpillar, Inc.
ChoicePoint, Inc.
Clarkston Consulting
ConocoPhillips
EDS
Fluor Corporation
Fuego
GE Healthcare
GE Advanced Materials
IBM Global Services
IBM Industry Groups
IBM Systems and Technology
iHealth Technologies
Infosys Technologies Limited
Insurity Inc.
McAfee, Inc.

MCI, Inc.
Microsoft Corporation
National Oilwell Varco, Inc.
NAVTEQ Corporation
New England Journal of Medicine
Nortel Networks Inc.
Northrop Grumman Corporation
SACHEM, Inc.
Salesforce.com
Schaller Anderson, Incorporated
Seagram Americas (now Diageo)
Shell
Siemens Business Communications
Siemens Business Services, GmbH & Co.
Sprint Corporation
Sun Microsystems, Inc.
Symantec Corp.
Symon Communications, Inc.
United States Golf Association
Vantage Partners, LLC
Vignette Corporation
Waste Management, Inc.

About the Authors

Mike Morton is managing partner and chief operating officer of CPS. He is responsible for the company's operations and consulting practices. Under his leadership, CPS has developed new product offerings and expanded its client list. Morton is also an in-demand facilitator at client workshops and strategy sessions.

Morton's 25-year career comprises executive management positions in finance, information systems, strategic planning, and mergers and acquisitions in the retail and materials industries. He co-founded a U.S.-based building and home improvement retailer, which subsequently was acquired by Kmart Corporation, and founded and served as president of a Texas-based, value-added reseller of IBM products and systems integrator.

Morton holds a graduate degree in business administration from the University of Denver in Denver, Colorado, and an undergraduate degree from the University of Mississippi.

After a 30-year career in sales, sales management, and senior executive management, CPS partner **Mike Higgins** is a widely recognized leadership authority and highly sought-after facilitator.

Higgins spent 14 years with IBM Corporation, where he served in sales, sales management, product management, and executive management. While in sales, he qualified for all nine of the One Hundred Percent Club annual awards for which he was eligible. As president of Cox Educational Services and managing partner of Brooks International, Higgins led the development and implementation of workplace education programs designed to address functional literacy and improve performance, specifically organizational redesign and change implementation. He also served as president of a full-service provider of maintenance and service for large mainframe-connected printing systems throughout Texas.

Higgins received an undergraduate degree in business administration from the University of North Texas in Denton, Texas, and a master's degree in international studies from Georgia State University in Atlanta, Georgia.

As CPS managing partner, Sales and Marketing, **Ken Evans** is responsible for the company's sales and marketing outreach. He also has primary responsibility for CPS' Chief Sales Officer Agenda consulting practice.

Evans' 25 years of diverse industry experience in sales, sales management, and executive management is a valuable resource in helping clients create successful selling organizations. A "reengineer," Evans led a $1-billion sales and service organization for IBM Corporation, and designed sales and service organizations and national accounts programs for Waste Management, Inc. In his next assignment, Evans consolidated six fluid power and motion control distribution companies and served as president of the new entity. He branded the enterprise, developed its go-to-market strategy, and instilled a sales and service culture to address customer business needs.

Evans earned a bachelor's degree from Washington and Lee University in Lexington, Virginia, and a master's degree in business administration from Southern Methodist University in Dallas, Texas.

Art Wilson founded Critical Path Strategies in 1992. A career-long student of corporate best practices, Wilson created the global consulting company to help clients identify and implement best practices of world-class selling organizations. His recognized knowledge and personal success in the sales arena are the foundation of CPS' customized sales processes, methodologies, and consulting offerings to enhance client-to-client and client-to-vendor effectiveness.

Prior to founding CPS, Wilson spent 23 years in sales and sales management with IBM Corporation. As an account manager, Wilson was recognized for five consecutive years as one of the top 10 sales representatives in IBM's 5,000-person U.S. sales force, including being named top salesperson one year.

Wilson holds an undergraduate degree in business administration from The University of Texas at Austin and a master's degree in business administration from St. Edward's University in Austin.

For more information on *Building a Successful Selling Organization* and Critical Path Strategies, visit our Web site at www.cpstrategy.com.

978-0-595-67343-8
0-595-67343-0

Printed in the United States
56059LVS00003BA/133-216